# MODERN
# ANTIQUES

## *for the Table*

# MODERN ANTIQUES

## *for the Table*

*A Complete
Guide to Tabletop
Accessories for Collecting
and Entertaining
1890–1940*

SHEILA CHEFETZ

*Photography by* JOSHUA GREENE

*Text by Risa Palazzo
Styling by Sara Scott Cullen*

*Penguin Studio Books*

*Life is about*

*shared memories.*

*This book is dedicated to those who preserved*

*and shared their memories with us, particu-*

*larly Ron Fox, Ivo Hadjiev, Tony Duquette,*

*and Carolyn Schnurer Noveck, who was my*

*first mentor and personal fairy godmother.*

*She invited me, aged twenty-three, to my*

*first glamorous New York dinner party and*

*twenty years later introduced me to Mike,*

*the husband with whom I've created*

*tomorrow's memories for our children*

*and grandchildren to share.*

PENGUIN STUDIO
Published by the Penguin Group
Penguin Putnam Inc,
375 Hudson Street,
New York, New York 10014, U.S.A.
Penguin Books Ltd,
27 Wrights Lane, London W8 5TZ,
England
Penguin Books Australia Ltd,
Ringwood, Victoria, Australia
Penguin Books Canada Ltd,
10 Alcorn Avenue, Toronto, Ontario,
Canada M4V 3B2
Penguin Books (N.Z.) Ltd,
182–190 Wairau Road, Auckland 10,
New Zealand
Penguin India,
210 Chiranjiv Tower, 43 Nehru Place,
New Delhi, India, 11009

Penguin Books Ltd,
Registered Offices:
Harmondsworth, Middlesex, England

First published in 1998 by Penguin Studio,
a member of Penguin Putnam Inc.
1 3 5 7 9 10 8 6 4 2
Copyright © Sheila Chefetz, 1998
Photographs copyright © Joshua Greene, 1998
All rights reserved

ISBN 0-670-87515-5
CIP data available
Printed in Singapore by Toppan Printing Co.
Set in Perpetua
Art Direction by Jaye Zimet
Designed by Renato Stanisic

# CONTENTS

# INTRODUCTION

This book is a continuation of the metaphorical "backward" journey that ends the introduction to my first book. Little did I realize that "the journey ahead" would take me to a variety of cities across the country, offering unexpected opportunities for exploring from diverse perspectives the side road of antiques for the table.

During this journey, tables were set with unlimited imagination in small towns as geographically diverse as Jonesboro, Arkansas, and Birmingham, Michigan, while favored antique objects became flower-filled centerpieces for luncheon tables in Shelby, North Carolina. At each book-lecture event I was stunned by the number of people (never fewer than three or four in the smallest town) who had already visited my shop in Great Barrington, Massachusetts, confirming my belief that true antiquers really are "time" travelers. Further affirmation comes from these words in a recent article in *The Magazine Antiques*: "With the popularization and affordability of the automobile, Americans took to the roads in great numbers, now able to search out antiques in heretofore inaccessible places." While they may have been looking for the primitive treasures of our colonial past, today's travelers are being exposed to "the antiques of tomorrow" (another phrase mentioned in the first book)—objects that will come of age, during their life span, in the next forty to fifty years. In fact, my first antiquing forays were the result of time travels on side roads near our weekend country house.

This book is about tableware antiques from approximately 1890 to 1940, offering a narrowly focused look back at the four principal areas of modern design and at the artisans, craftsmen, industry, and social leaders who defined fifty years of enormous productivity and creativity, and began what was to become The American Century. In fact, the two cities I've chosen as backdrops for this book were the two "pulse points" of America: one, Detroit, provided the industry; the other, Los Angeles, the fantasy. They gave us, and the world, the car and the movies; mobility and aspirations available to all. Having been a child born during the Great Depression, I remember nickel-admission movies in which glamorous people in "modern" dwellings had "dinner at eight" and drank martinis. I also remember our car's being the family's Sunday passport to a day free of work and spent visiting, eating, and playing cards with grandparents, aunts, uncles, and cousins. So a good number of the antique styles illustrated in this book were actually part of my life or memory, often causing me an intense case of déjà vu.

The feeling of "having been there before" surfaced many times in the course of my journeys, culminating one evening at The Whitney Restaurant in Detroit, where I was introduced to Ron Fox, an owner, who is the unofficial social historian and restorer emeritus of Detroit. He generously offered to give me a backstage tour of the 1894 and virtually intact house that had metamorphosed into a fine dining landmark. One glimpse of the original Tiffany windows, Art Nouveau wrought-iron staircase, rare Minton-tile fireplace surround, and Ron's enthusiastically knowledgeable show-and-tell of the antique tablewares he had collected over a thirty-year period is the reason this book began that night in Detroit. Ron's descriptions of pieces included a history of the family that owned them, how they entertained, set the table, traveled, married and divorced, or even scandalized society. As the friend and frequent companion of Anna Thompson Dodge, who was a fabled international hostess of her day, he has saved documents, clothes, letters, gifts, and tablewares from her estate. Although many of the objects were not yet officially antique, they represented the best of an era when constant change became the norm.

California, a state wholly dependent on the automobile, chronicled that change, providing movie screens full of design information scripted or art-directed by creative immigrants seeking freedom between two world wars. This was recently chronicled by the superb "Exiles and Emigrés" show at the Los Angeles County Museum of Art. European culture and taste, often avant-garde, came to America and then interpreted, idealized, and aggrandized America to the rest of the world. Moorish castles, Italian villas, French châteaux, and Norman cottages cropped up along America's West Coast. If one had a fantasy, why not build it in California, where there was plenty of room and more than enough sunshine and palm trees. Movies, cars, houses, furnishings, and table settings were all bigger than life. I've lectured more in California than elsewhere, and during these visits I've been invited to explore unique properties and collections. The Robinson House in Beverly Hills, an Italian-style villa filled with an eclectic mix of Virginia Robinson's furnishings, is one such wonderful example, enhanced by Ivo Hadjiev, the deceased Mrs. Robinson's last household majordomo, who still lives in the house, caring for her fine collection. His recollections bring each piece to life, adding as much luster to Virginia Robinson's character as the silver polish does to the objects he works on. Both Ivo and Ron are treasures, because they have been recording and preserving social history for others to draw on, learn from, and enjoy. Although neither man has studied to be an art historian, each brings insightful awareness of surrounding political, social, and artistic influences into their remembrances.

Having studied art history as part of my fashion-design curriculum in college, I have always been fascinated by the interconnection of events and by the artistic talents that respond to those external stimuli. The flow of creative ideas from country to country

and the ways in which one school of thought or design cross-pollinates with others are other aspects of that history that interest me. I want this book to focus on the design concepts and the designers of tablewares, rather than the uses and basic manufacturing processes, spanning a much wider time frame, that were discussed in my first book. Although our starting point is roughly 1890, one cannot discuss the Arts and Crafts Movement and a 1905 Greene and Greene House without explaining the ripple effect from the 1893 World's Columbian Exposition in Chicago, the Aesthetic movement of the 1870s, and, of course, Admiral Perry's opening up of Japan in 1853–1854, the original stone in the water. I can feel those connected threads when I hold a rippled-Martelé piece of American silver in the Japanese Aesthetic style; it is a tangible, everyday, usable link to the power and endurance of good design, which can harmonize with and enhance well-designed tablewares of any era. Although we tried to place some objects in houses and environments of the same period, we never felt that we should try to re-create history. We used creative license, and you should too, by bringing your own personality into the mix, just as our documented hostesses did in their day.

In some cases, the objects we've photographed were held by some very famous hands; Prime Minister Anthony Eden came for tea, and Mrs. Robinson poured from her prized silver service, while Mr. and Mrs. Edsel Ford hosted Washington's power elite or visiting Hollywood stars. Other pieces, no less prized, once enhanced the lives of anonymous owners, and are now doing the same for knowledgeable collectors of limited means. Anna Thompson Dodge purchased Catherine the Great's fabled pearls, as well as the most expensive Steuben stemware, while Matilda Dodge Wilson, her sister-in-law, often dined alone surrounded by the sumptuous splendor of the finest wood-paneling and carving in the sixty-foot Christopher Wren–style dining room of Meadow

Brook Hall, the fourth-largest house in America. Being allowed to view, photograph, and set the table with her superb silver, porcelain, and glasswares with the knowledgeable, enthusiastic help of Paul McDowell was indeed a privilege. Unimagined insights, visual surprises, and unusual discoveries added to the satisfaction of working on this project. In their stately English Tudor manor house, the Edsel Fords had Walter Dorwin Teague design "a modern room," still intact, to showcase their collection of African-American art, African artifacts, and walls and furnishings crafted from a variety of African woods. While having lunch in California, I casually mentioned to Phoebe Vaccaro that we had photographed while in Detroit a piece of President Rutherford B. Hayes's dinner service. She replied, "Well, then, I have a letter from him [to her grandmother] at home in my drawer; perhaps you'd like to photograph that, too!" Good fortune and photographs are the result of such serendipitous coincidence. A day our team will never forget was spent at Tony Duquette's fantasy house, where the table was set with a mélange of his favorite things surrounded by the splendor of his wildly exotic, terraced, Asian-jungle garden. After photographing it, we were invited to be seated and enjoy a most delicious lunch, listening to Tony's and Hutton's stories of "old Hollywood" and about Tony's collaborative work with the famous decorator Elsie de Wolfe (who later became Lady Mendl), and as a studio set designer for *The Ziegfeld Girl* and others of that era's great American musical extravaganzas.

All of us are indebted to Hutton Wilkinson, Tony's business partner and friend, who orchestrated that memorable day and capped it by allowing us to photograph his exquisite pool and jewel-box dining room, each set to express his own distinctive style.

I haven't yet explained the reason for our third location, The Greenbrier Hotel in White Sulphur Springs, West Virginia, or the fact that it was actually where the first photographs for this book were taken. In the early planning stages, I wanted to take a tour of America's grand hotels and resorts in part to show how travel, cars, and newfound industrial wealth affected a growing upper class. Since I was to be a guest lecturer at The Greenbrier, I requested permission for Joshua Greene and me to do our test shoot at the hotel. We accomplished so much there that we decided it would stand as the prototype for the other "Grands" of the early twentieth century. It has endured and thrived while many others have disappeared.

As I have written, this has been a most rewarding journey, taking me aboard Barbara Hutton's long-idled private railroad car; allowing me to walk the deck on board the venerable *Queen Mary,* which is now a floating hotel/museum at Long Beach, California, and to explore the archival treasures five decks down in the ship's hold; and enabling me to run my hands over the silver monogram on Edsel Ford's favorite Lincoln. All of this came about because I like to set the table, poke through drawers and closets, and sit enthralled while people like Ron, Ivo, and others I've met on the road fill in the histories that magically bring our make-believe feasts to life. I hope their shared knowledge and insights add a special glow and dimension to the "modern" tablewares, which, while still findable, practical, and affordable, can infuse today's dining experience with tactile pleasures. Using objects created during a fertile fifty years of design experimentation that reflected the talents, technology, optimism, and freedom that were defined in those early years of a new century will give continued comfort and familiarity to the next millennium. As we journey forward, we can't help wanting to look back, touch, and remember. Now I'd like you, our reader, to be my guest at this interpretation of half a century of progressive decorative arts design, viewed from the perspective of the "best table in the house."

# Art Nouveau

A TOULOUSE-LAUTREC POSTER OF THE CANCAN DANCERS AT THE MOULIN-ROUGE, A TIFFANY LAMP, THE ENTRANCES TO THE MÉTRO SUBWAY IN PARIS, AND THE TWIST AND TANGLE OF A CLUSTER OF IRISES WINDING THEIR WAY UP TOWARD THE SUN ALL CAPTURE THE ESSENCE OF ART NOUVEAU—THE DARINGLY EXOTIC DECORATIVE ARTS MOVEMENT THAT LIVED BRIEFLY FROM ABOUT 1890 TO 1915 AND STILL CAPTIVATES US TODAY, ALMOST A CENTURY LATER.

WHAT THESE FOUR WORKS OF ART AND NATURE SHARE IS A LOVE AFFAIR WITH THE UNDULATING LINE; FOR, ABOVE EVERYTHING ELSE, ART NOUVEAU WAS ABOUT CURVES AND SWIRLS, SPINNING AND WINDING AND QUIVERING WITH LIFE. EVERY SINU-OUS TWIST SUGGESTED THE ORGANIC SHAPES OF NATURE EVEN AS THEY WERE EXAGGERATED, ELONGATED, AND STRETCHED UNTIL THEY BECAME ALMOST CARICATURES OF THEIR TRUE SELVES. FLOWERS LANGUIDLY DOZED ON THE ENDS OF THIN, LONG

**PRECEDING PAGES:** *In a dining room that is pure Art Nouveau, a poster by H.G. Ibels creates an unmistakably Belle Époque ambiance. On the table is a centerpiece composed of two exquisite Gallé vases and an alabaster bust, together with Reed and Barton's 1904 Modern Art flatware pattern, citrine and green Art Nouveau etched stemware with funnel-twist stems, and Austrian Art Nouveau gilded plates that capture the ambiance of turn-of-the-century Paris.*

**OPPOSITE, ABOVE, AND RIGHT:** *Encompassing Art Nouveau's decorative arts, this dining room wallpapered in William Morris's 1892 pattern Black Thorn is set for a formal dinner party with a German Jugendstil epergne, Haviland orchid-decorated plates, and six different Art Nouveau silver place settings from one collection.*

stems barely emerging from reluctantly opening pale green buds, butterflies encircled sunflowers heavy and drooping with nectar—all under the watchful eye of a sky filled with billowing clouds.

Art Nouveau's lines danced around art-pottery vases, outlined the painstakingly crafted pieces of stained glass from which the style would become famous, and whiplashed back onto themselves like snakes uncertain of which path to take; vines slithered up and down staircase banisters and wound around candlesticks and the rims of glasses in an exuberant exultation of the natural world.

Glassmakers, silversmiths, and ceramics designers reveled in the aesthetic possibilities posed by the new style and created startling objects for the home. The dining table particularly benefited from the wide array of decorative pieces that flooded the market during the opulent Belle Époque, providing the homemaker with tantalizing

choices: a bronze sculpture of a young maiden with cascading hair or a Steuben glass vase enveloped by silver leaves and filled with peacock feathers could be used as a sophisticated centerpiece; Gien or Coalport porcelain plates decorated with highly stylized tulips or a turbulent ocean wave might be framed by Gorham silver flatware with whimsically sculpted floral handles; Tiffany iridescent glasses could pop up like shimmering mauve-colored tulips from a linen cloth hand-embroidered with yellow lilies; and a bottle of Perrier-Jouët champagne could chill in a Whiting silver ice bucket delicately engraved with stalks of bamboo or gracefully wading herons.

During the fin de siècle, or the Gilded Age, as it was named by Mark Twain, the earth seemed to spin a little faster than usual as it jet-

**OPPOSITE:** *Fleurette tea and coffee pots of about 1910 by Burleigh emulate real life in useful versions of Art Nouveau style.*

**ABOVE:** *Art and nature are combined in aesthetically stylized bone-handled serving pieces and a highly stylized turtle-decorated soup bowl.*

tisoned itself into a brand-new century. The era was blessed with great economic prosperity that created a steady flow of money through an unusually peaceful Europe. The French movement that would eventually become known as Art Nouveau grew out of this serene and affluent time.

James Abbott McNeill Whistler, Alphonse Mucha, Gustav Klimt, Toulouse-Lautrec, Aubrey Beardsley, Oscar Wilde, Émile Gallé, Louis Majorelle, Louis Comfort Tiffany, and scores of other creative souls beat a path into the uncharted territory of a style that had no antecedent. Beardsley's provocative illustrations, with their themes of depravity and perversion, and Wilde's dandified dress and then-scandalous lifestyle became synonymous with a style of art that advocated the pursuit of beauty above all else—an art for art's sake.

Oscar Wilde, in particular, had a profound influence on the Art Nouveau style: his fondness for lilies (rumored to have grown out of his admiration for the legendary society beauty Lillie Langtry) kindled the enthusiasm for the lily as a decorative motif during the period, and his predilection for arranging peacock feathers instead of flowers in his rooms began a trend. Wilde's penchant for collecting fine old porcelain led him to lament, "Oh, would that I could live up to my blue-and-white china!" and spurred like-minded enthusiasts to depart on "antiquing expeditions" in search of similar wares.

Art Nouveau, or New Art, was the modest name chosen by the French for a decorative style that was revolutionary in its time. And it was new in every sense of the word: original, modern, distinctive, and, yes, even bizarre. Of course, advocates of the style preferred "distinctive," while adversaries most certainly opted for "bizarre."

The direct origin of the name "Art Nouveau" was the art connoisseur Samuel Bing's Paris shop, La Maison de l'Art Nouveau; this is where the great actress Sarah Bernhardt shopped for Lalique jewelry and ordered Mucha posters to advertise her theatrical performances, and where the china, glass, and silver of the finest craftsmen of the day could be purchased. Bing saw the style as a way to offer "a return to divine Nature, always fresh and new in her counsels," and he was at once a patron and a skilled businessman who must be credited with cultivating a movement that might have perished without him. He promoted Art Nouveau when other shop owners were too timid to

**OPPOSITE, ABOVE:** *An Art Nouveau vase made by J. F. Catain in 1916; and* **BELOW:** *a 1910 demitasse cup and saucer by J.P.L., Limoges.*

**BELOW:** *This superb Whiting silver punch bowl and ladle with repoussé enamel work and grapevine detailing was originally made at the turn of the century as a presentation gift to an English lord.*

*The Art Nouveau influence is evident in the delicate silver overlay on this porcelain demitasse set by Paragon circa 1925, which is displayed on a child's "ladies" chair.*

commit themselves to a style often referred to as "decadent" by hostile critics, who blamed Art Nouveau for everything from bad taste to the downfall of civilization.

Tiffany and Bing's symbiotic relationship began in 1895 when Tiffany manufactured ten stained-glass windows designed by Toulouse-Lautrec and Pierre Bonnard for La Maison de l'Art Nouveau. Bing was eager to represent America's foremost decorative artist in Paris, and Tiffany was at last assured a prominent agent through whose gallery his work would reach the overseas audience he lacked.

Despite its French heart, Art Nouveau did manage to thrive in a number of Europe's capitals; much like a chameleon, the style subtly changed its appearance as it slithered across national borders and mountain chains. In Germany it was called Youth Style (Jugendstil) and Lily Style; Italians called it Liberty Style (after the London shop) and Noodle Style; in Belgium it was Eel Style, while in Austria it was called the Viennese Secession.

Louis Comfort Tiffany defined Art Nouveau for Americans who might have ignored the movement otherwise. Before he became known for his spectacular lamp designs, Tiffany developed a large following as an interior designer who extensively used decorative tiles and stained-glass windows in his work. In 1894, the lumber baron David Whitney, Jr., commissioned Tiffany to make a number of stained-glass panels for his Detroit mansion, one of the most elaborate residences in this part of the country at the time. Although Romanesque in its overall design, it contained, in addition to Tiffany's windows and a fine set of Minton tiles, a great number of Art Nouveau decorative pieces that would become priceless collectibles dur-

**RIGHT:** *Wonderful examples of 1903 Tiffany Favrile glass—a graceful tulip vase and compote.*

**OPPOSITE, ABOVE:** *This splendid Art Nouveau lamp circa 1910 has a beautiful shell clasped and supported by a sinuous bronze base.*

**OPPOSITE, BELOW:** *Bronze gilt over Favrile glass vase, designed in the Moorish style by Louis Comfort Tiffany.*

ing a brief, dizzying revival of Art Nouveau in the late 1960s and early 1970s. Perhaps it was the psychedelic-like swirls, daring color combinations, and conspicuous pursuit of pleasure that had defined the fin de siècle that rekindled a particularly passionate romance with the movement at this free-spirited time in America's history. The artist Peter Max was especially successful at blending Art Nouveau shapes with contemporary themes, and Wilde's ruffled shirts and velvet suits became au courant once again.

Although the style meant different things to different people, there was one unifying thread that ran throughout, pulling it together—the decorative influence of Japan. This influence can be observed in Whistler's painting *La Princesse du pays de la porcelaine,* in which he shamelessly borrowed Japanese art techniques, and also in

*Modern Antiques for the Table*

a new preference for asymmetrical pattern placement on plates and ceramic vases, which had long been a feature of Oriental design. The fascination with Japonisme, while apparent in many of Art Nouveau's best-known works, was shared by other movements as well, particularly the concurrent Arts and Crafts Movement in England and the United States.

It is important to understand that the turn of the century was not monopolized by one movement: there was a constant cross-fertilization of ideas that allowed for the simultaneous existence of competing movements—from Art Nouveau, Revivalism, and Arts and Crafts, to the Art Deco style that developed in the 1920s—all of which influenced tableware design in Europe and America during the period from about 1890 through the early 1940s.

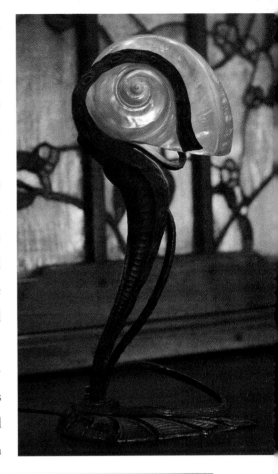

The overlapping of ideas that constituted these various movements was most evident at the multitude of international exhibitions held during the period. These giant, often glass-enclosed, noisy, and crowded extravaganzas presented the very latest in the arts and in technology to the masses and brought creative minds together under one roof, so an English silversmith could see the work of an Italian glassblower, who could, in turn, see the work of a French potter. Art's inability to thrive in a vacuum and its dependence on the reactions and input of fellow artists made exhibitions and world fairs particularly fertile breeding grounds for artistic ideas.

The greatest showcase for Art Nouveau was unquestionably the Exposition Universelle held in Paris in 1900, for it was there that the greatest existing and aspiring designers in the field, most notably Émile Gallé and Louis Comfort Tiffany, displayed their wares on the banks of the Seine and made Art

The spectacular Tiffany windows capture the exuberant spirit of the Art Nouveau movement and a dramatic mix of tablewares, including colored Venetian trumpet-shaped stemware, enamel-and-gold floral medallion plates, and Reed and Barton's cut-crystal-and-silver claret jugs.

OPPOSITE, BELOW: The luminous beauty of a Favrile wineglass circa 1900 echoes the stained-glass window by Tiffany.

Nouveau a fashionable and economically viable style.

Just as the builders and designers of Art Nouveau were a new breed, so were its customers: the industrialization of Western Europe had created a wealthy group of individuals, the nouveau riche, who wanted pretty things for the home. And in America, a newly formed middle class was anxious to define itself apart from the recent immigrants; what better way to do this than with a finely furnished home appointed with beautiful china, glassware, and silver on the table?

While a complete Art Nouveau residence as advocated by the purists of the style might have been too much of a good thing for the average citizen, people were eager to bring bits and pieces in the form of decorative objects into their homes: perhaps a stunning Tiffany candelabrum; a set of china with elongated teacups nipped in at the waist like the corseted dresses of the time; or a silver serpent-entwined bowl by Gorham or Reed and Barton. Art Nouveau's playful patterns were particularly well suited to two-dimensional surface effects, and it was for this reason that its beauty was better expressed in America by glassmakers,

**ABOVE:** *Many silver companies produced distinctive floral-motif patterns. Illustrated here* **RIGHT** *are the Dauphin pattern by Durgin circa 1897 and* **LEFT** *Lily by Whiting.*

**BELOW:** *A variety of salad servers span the styles of modern antiques we explore in this book. Included here is a set appliquéd with bronze, gold, and copper by George W. Shiebler, Wallace's Art Deco pattern from 1917, Whiting's 1902 Lily pattern, and Comstock by Shreve and Company.*

silversmiths, and ceramics designers than it was by architects—although in Paris, Barcelona, and Prague many pure Art Nouveau buildings were erected that are still standing today.

Malleable glass—capable of being molded, cut, engraved, colored, or layered—was a medium, perhaps more than any other, made for Art Nouveau. Tiffany, working closely with the designer Arthur Nash, created spectacular new surface effects in glass. His fascination with the iridescent look of many of the ancient Roman objects he collected led him to his most-heralded invention—Favrile glass. Through the ingenious application of a solution of metallic vapors to colored glass, Tiffany was able to mimic the appearance of centuries-old glass, creating what Samuel Bing referred to as "a delicate, silky epidermis" that would be often imitated yet never duplicated. Today, just one of Tiffany's magnificent Favrile-glass vases, perhaps filled with a bunch of tulips or one splendid lily, brings a touch of the Gay Nineties to even the most contemporary table.

Tiffany's studio worked the full range of popular motifs of the day—peacocks, flowers, plants, roots, stems, vines, and Japanese shapes and patterns—into a huge array of decorative art glass and tableware that, in addition to being beautiful, helped raise the status of America as a design force in the world; Tiffany's designs captured the imagination of Europeans, who were enthralled by the technical skills he used to express his

**ABOVE:** *A Japanese enameled teapot, sugar, and creamer capture the delicate beauty of nature on silver.*

**BELOW:** *Like molten silver, Art Nouveau swirls cover a circa 1900 silver crumber by Derby, an American silver maker.*

seemingly limitless imagination. His windows, lamps, stemware, and vases were coveted in countries that had long been dominated by European artists and craftsmen.

Although Tiffany's creations were of first importance, he was not alone in fabricating Art Nouveau glass that still intrigues and mesmerizes contemporary collectors. Steuben Glass hired Frederick Carder, an Englishman, who helped develop a line of iridescent glass called Aurene, which closely resembled Tiffany's Favrile and is very beautiful indeed. In Austria, Johannes Loetz used asymmetrical forms executed in combinations of opaque colors and silvery-blue splashed patterns applied to brilliant cobalt or green grounds, and also specialized in applying trailing handles that surrounded the bodies of their vessels in a whimsical and innovative way.

Though the turn of the century would be most heralded for its art glass, the period was also marked by a still healthy appetite for the heavily cut and etched glass so adored by the Victorians. Innumerable patterns were precisely cut into rich blue- or yellow-tinted glass decanters and stemware, often further embellished with swirling motifs. An innovation that caught fire with the public was glass onto which a thin overlay of silver, usually in flowing botanical patterns, was electroplated and further emphasized by engraved or etched details. Loetz and Steuben enjoyed great success with this particular technique, and often used it for their vases and water carafes.

Through an unprecedented number of ingenious innovations in the manufacture of glass developed during the late nineteenth century, many manufacturers made their glass impersonate myriad other materials; mother-of-pearl, satin, and gold are only some of the guises Art Nouveau art glass adopted.

In France, the finest glass was made in Nancy—for this was where Émile Gallé established his factory in 1884. By now, after reading about the fascination with nature shared by the Art Nouveau designers, you should not be surprised to learn that Émile Gallé was a trained botanist. His love of the environment was expressed in the sentiment "Our roots are in the depths of the woods, beside the springs, among the mosses," which was inscribed above the door of his studio. Gallé combined his encyclopedic knowledge of plants and his love of Symbolist literature to make his highly entertaining *verres parlants* (talking glasses), which were etched with lines from his favorite poems. His use of cameo glass was inspired, and was much copied by rival glassmakers, such as the Daum brothers.

China underwent a far less radical change during the turn of the century than did glass. This may be because there was no great style-defining talent to attract the attention of the public; or it may be because, by its very nature, china doesn't have the sparkle or the color of glass. Its charms are expressed in a quieter way, demurely gleaming under the light of a candlelit centerpiece or drawing the eye slowly around a delicately painted border. During the Art Nouveau period, china companies in Europe and America experimented with glazes and shapes to create new designs that would be used mostly on decorative wares such as vases and bowls, called art pottery, rather than on more useful wares, such as plates and cups for the dining table. Still, Art Nouveau border patterns and unique shapes were designed and adapted to mass-production methods to create tableware that was in step with current tastes.

Coalport and Tiffany added Moorish-style designs to some of their dishes to compete with France's large commercial factories like Sèvres, Vincennes, and many Limoges makers, who were also beginning to produce Art Nouveau–inspired tableware. Flower-bedecked maidens were lavishly painted onto porcelain, as were Japanese images, and there was even a surge of interest in hand-

*Coalport's stunning beaded-edge, hand-painted floral paisley plates enhance this table setting together with Bavarian embossed service plates, a silver-overlay vase and decanter by Loetz, Morgantown cobalt-blue goblets and citron swirl-cut wineglasses, and Reed and Barton Pointed Antique silver.*

painting china as a lucrative hobby among the homemakers of the time.

In England, the ceramics community found the various revival styles and their own Aesthetic and Arts and Crafts movements more compelling than Art Nouveau, although Coalport did produce a number of lines with motifs suggestive of the French style. Wedgwood's interest in Art Nouveau lasted well into the 1920s with the manufacture of a line called Dragon Lustre or Fairyland Lustre; these wares were adapted from Chinese and Japanese ceramics, and featured a variety of beautiful colors and mottled luster finishes.

Minton, influenced by the Viennese Secession style, produced art pottery with straplike or sinuous handles, with stylized floral motifs in enamel colors of lilac, turquoise, green, and crimson outlined in raised paste gold; the large earthenware plaques were excellent vehicles for the unconstrained Aesthetic style, and the table china incorporated seminude maidens often posed against a background of peacock feathers, as well as slip-trailed and molded plates.

During the Art Nouveau period, as always, both useful and decorative objects were produced from silver, but less precious metals, such as copper, pewter, wrought iron, and brass, were used as well. The methods of decoration included chasing, embossing, applying metal on metal, and the practice of inlaying semiprecious stones into Art Nouveau forms. In France, bronze and gilded-metal statuettes modeled after the dancer Loie Fuller were made by Alexandre Charpentier, Eugene Feuillatre, and Théodore Rivière, making her somewhat of a "poster girl" for the style.

Although many Americans were reluctant to purchase a set of silver flatware that might be out of style in a few years, Tiffany & Co. did produce Art Nouveau flatware lines called Japanese, Vine, and Lap Over Edge as well as dessert services that featured spoons, forks, and knives with all-different flower handles. Many of their larger decorative pieces for the table, including punch bowls, were displayed at the World's Columbian Exposition in Chicago in 1893, the Exposition Universelle in Paris in 1900, and the Pan-American Exposition in Buffalo in 1901. Islamic art, particularly the art of Persia and Turkey, interested Tiffany's and they made a number of long-necked coffeepots influenced by these regions. Scarabs and other Egyptian motifs, in general favor during the late nineteenth century, had particular appeal for Tiffany, who had visited Egypt as early as 1870, and he used them in much of his small silver table-ware; in addition, images of the American West, popularized by Buffalo Bill's touring Wild West shows, occasionally appeared in Tiffany's work. Shiebler and Gorham applied insects and sea creatures of contrasting metals to the surfaces of their wares; they also used leaves, cattails, and animals (some of them inspired by Rudyard Kipling's *The Jungle Book*) in a naturalistic style. William Codman of Gorham excelled in low bowls with sensuous curves and nature-based chased decorations.

The greatest movements in art and design are those that have etched in our minds two or three works that convey, in one clear masterstroke, precisely what the movement wanted to say; while Toulouse-Lautrec and Tiffany certainly managed to do just that, Art Nouveau would soon yield to changing tastes. It may be argued that Art Nouveau became a victim of its adamant rejection of the past; that had it been less driven by a desire to realize such an extreme change, it might have enjoyed a longer life than it did during the turn of the last century. And yet, it is precisely those elements that may have alienated an audience still holding fast to Victorian tastes—such as Art Nouveau's erotic subjects and flamboyant use of line—that captivate us today.

*Peacock colors create an exotic blend of decoration for a table at The Whitney, which is set in front of the stunning Minton tiles of the library's fireplace. A Victorian silk fringed shawl becomes a dramatic tablecloth.*

# ARTS & CRAFTS

THE SAME RESTLESS DESIRE FOR CHANGE THAT BREATHED LIFE INTO THE ART NOUVEAU STYLE IN FRANCE HELPED TO SPAWN A SISTER STYLE, ARTS AND CRAFTS, IN ENGLAND. MUCH LIKE REAL SIBLINGS, THEY RESEMBLED EACH OTHER IN MANY WAYS, YET DISTINCTIONS IN ATTITUDE AND POINT OF VIEW GAVE THEM EACH AN INDIVIDUAL PERSONALITY, AND THEY BLOSSOMED INTO TWO INDEPENDENT MOVEMENTS THAT PRODUCED TABLEWARES INFUSED WITH AN ENERGY THAT HAS NOT BEEN STILLED EVEN A CENTURY AFTER THEY WERE MADE. A FUNDAMENTAL DIFFER-ENCE BETWEEN THE TWO STYLES THAT INSTANTLY DISTIN-GUISHES AN ART NOUVEAU OBJECT FROM ONE MADE BY A PROPONENT OF ARTS AND CRAFTS IS FOUND IN THEIR VERY DIVERSE AP-PROACHES TO THE USE OF LINE AS A MEANS OF REPRE-SENTING NATURE; THE SEN-SUOUS LINES AND FEMININE CURVES THAT WERE SO MUCH A PART OF THE FRENCH STYLE MET WITH

limited success in England, where a cleaner, more simplified depiction of nature was strongly favored. A point of agreement between the two styles was their mutual love of Japonisme, yet each gleaned different elements from Japan's wealth of dramatic design motifs and gave them a Western twist. While the exotic "whiplash" lines and subject matter found in much Japanese artwork was emulated by the French, the English were most intrigued by the bold colors, unusual perspective, and sparseness of decoration used by the Japanese.

The Arts and Crafts Movement emerged in the final quarter of the nineteenth century under the tutelage of two men—the philosopher and art critic John Ruskin, and the designer and poet William Morris. Each offered sound reasons for a return to the higher morals and pride in craftsmanship exemplified by medieval craft guilds. Both Ruskin and Morris warned that the tedium of factory work that had become the norm during the Industrial Revolution was damaging the very souls of workers by destroying any incentive to create objects of true beauty and worth, made with the heart as well as the hand. Each man dreamed of raising the quality

**PRECEDING PAGES:** *At Cranbrook House, the rich colors and textures of the Arts and Crafts Movement assemble in front of a fireplace made by the Pewabic Tile Company of Detroit. The small vases in front of a row of Minton plates on the mantel were also made by Pewabic. The richly marbled-glaze dinner plate is by Royal Doulton.*
**INSET** *A mosaic floor highlights a 1920s William Morris-inspired dinner plate by Royal Doulton and an 1880s Derby Moorish-tile pattern made for Tiffany & Co.*

**OPPOSITE:** *This is part of the masterful dining room at the Gamble House in Pasadena, with its original furnishings, lighting fixtures, and stained-glass panels designed by Greene and Greene.*

**ABOVE AND RIGHT:** *An interplay of colors and textures is created at the Gamble House with Royal Fan china, a 1920s pattern by Stevens and Williams, and Whiting's Honeysuckle flatware. The yellow and gold glass picks up the colors of the camellia centerpiece, while Chinese artifacts from the Gamble collection add Oriental whimsy.*

**LEFT AND ABOVE:** *Thomas Hart Benton's landscape* Dreaming at the Pond *and an oil by Frank Myers offer a colorful accompaniment to the Storer House dining room designed by Frank Lloyd Wright. The china is a reproduction of the service that Wright designed for the Imperial Hotel in Japan. Along with original Wright salt and pepper shakers and flatware designed by Charles Rennie Mackintosh these eye-catching plates sit on a table designed by the famed architect. Four sizes of stemware by Dorothy Thorpe, silver Arts and Crafts napkin rings, and bronze Jarvie candlesticks complete this splendid table setting assembled by the owner.*

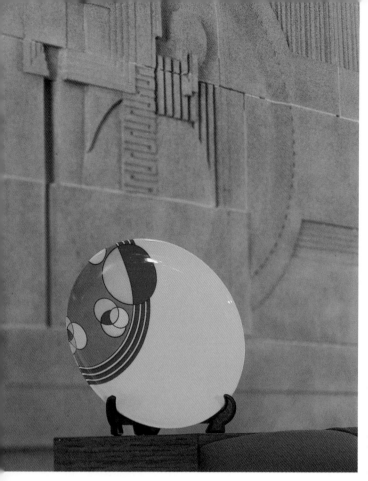

of the decorative arts to a level comparable with that of fine painting and sculpture; since many designers and reformers both in England and elsewhere were appalled by the glut of inferior machine-made goods churned out on a daily basis, the message of Ruskin and Morris struck a resounding chord and instigated the emergence of such highly esteemed workshops as Charles Eastlake's, and Charles Ashbee's Guild of Handicraft.

Scotland's premier architect/designer team, Charles Rennie Mackintosh and his wife, Margaret McDonald, while adhering to the movement's insistence on a totality of design that linked interiors to exteriors, managed brilliantly to bring their own voice to the Arts and Crafts style. Mackintosh created homes and tea shops in Glasgow that fused the geometry inherent in much of Arts and Crafts design with an attention to intensely pretty details, like stained-glass panels dancing with roses and hearts, which still look astonishingly fresh as we approach the twenty-first century. The rooms that he and his wife decorated

**ABOVE:** *Coordinates by Frank Lloyd Wright, a series of bright graphic designs, show the designer's visionary concept of mix-and-match china-pattern interplays similar to the way that he patterned concrete walls with gold and luster squares and used leaded-glass windows to echo the stylized design of Hollyhock House.*

**RIGHT:** *A Frank Lloyd Wright demitasse set made by Royal Worcester explored the use of colorful graphic designs and modern shapes for tablewares.*

**OPPOSITE:** *Charlotte Rhead's early 1920s demitasse set, anticipating modernism, has a fruit design inspired by the 1914 Brunswick pool table at the Lanterman House.*

**LEFT:** *An Aesthetic Movement botanical study in earth colors on a dinner plate and soup tureen from the 1880s.*

*From 1908, a hand-painted bowl and underplate by Kent shares a table with one of the period's most popular flowers, the lily.*

**ABOVE:** *Reindeer are invited to this aesthetically cozy lunch next to the fire. William Morris coordinated fabrics, china by Hall and Read, green gilded pressed glass, and touches of ivory are used to make a rustic table setting.*

**OPPOSITE:** *Royal Worcester Orlando china from 1928, while more Beaux Arts in design, mixes well with Whiting's Aesthetic 1880s–1890s Japanese pattern flatware, a fork and knife of parcel gilt on sterling and mixed-metal dinner knife by Gorham, making an autumnal table setting in a silver collector's small Mission house.*

for their own home were pale perfection; done up in delicate white, they would blend in splendidly at any one of today's trendiest designer showcases. In fact, Charles Rennie Mackintosh is enjoying a revival of sorts now, with architecture and design students flocking to see his work, examples of which were recently shown at exhibitions held in his honor at many of the world's largest museums.

A yearning among the population at large to return to more innocent and bucolic times before the almighty machine was switched on made the Arts and Crafts Movement very successful, particularly in England, where the Industrial Revolution was born, but America embraced Arts and Crafts designs as well, and the movement evolved here from 1890 to 1920 even if it did metamorphose into a style that differed markedly from that of its British counterpart. After visiting England, where they were introduced to the Arts and Crafts philosophy as taught by Morris and Ruskin, the Americans Elbert Hubbard and Gustav Stickley returned to New York State and set up their own artist communities, called, respectively, Roycroft and United Crafts, where they could teach the style that had so profoundly won them over—with one very important difference: while the English leaders of the movement despised the machines they had seen turn out so many crass goods, both Hubbard and Stickley embraced the use of machines for doing work that they were particularly well suited for, while leaving ample room for the expressive handiwork that was the trademark of the style.

Known as a philosophy for good living as well as a decorative style, the Arts and Crafts Movement advocated that people take a greater responsibility for their good health, through proper nutrition, sufficient exercise, and plenty of fresh air and sunshine. Americans, in particular, took the movement's admonitions very much to heart, and a great many people set off to the mountains, to the seashore, and to California, where a great fondness for the style resulted in more Arts and Crafts–style bungalows than anywhere else in the country. At the same time, the many three-hundred-year-old Spanish missions that were a part of the Western and Southwestern landscape inspired California's newest settlers to adapt some of the flavor of these buildings to their own homes, and the Mission style, a subset of Arts and Crafts, was born. On the way out west, the Arts and Crafts Movement left its mark on the Midwest as well, where the style was called Prairie, in reference to the surrounding landscape; regional designers established their own societies to promote the style both in architecture and in furnishings for the interior of the home.

The tenets of Arts and Crafts extended to many other parts of the globe, including Scandinavia, where the Danish silversmith Georg Jensen's flatware and hollowware designs would span decades, and styles from Arts and Crafts to Art Deco and Moderne. In addition, the Finnish architect Eliel Saarinen, who is credited with being one of the earliest leaders of the movement, was eventually invited to America, where he continued his work and taught at the Cranbrook Academy in Bloomfield Hills, Michigan. In Austria the designers Josef Hoffmann and Koloman Moser, who had founded in 1893 their country's version of France's Art Nouveau, called the Viennese Secession, abandoned it in 1903 to form a new group, the Wiener Werkstätte, which drew inspiration from England's Arts and Crafts movement to produce a wide range of innovative china, silver, and glassware that still looks modern to us today.

In America, the style was perhaps best expressed in architecture, and a number of new home designs evolved: the bungalow, a low-slung structure with deep eaves, adapted from the small houses built by nineteenth-century British colonial officers in India; the Prairie School house, which was characterized by an open floor plan and an extensive use of brick and

concrete; and the Craftsman house, popularized through Gustav Stickley's magazine, *The Craftsman*. Preeminent among American architects working in an Arts and Crafts–inspired style were two brothers from Ohio, Charles and Henry Greene, who built houses that defined the movement in form and spirit—most notably, the Gamble House in Pasadena, California, which provides a wonderfully rich background for some of the photographs in this book and stands as a living testament to the Greenes' inspired work. While the brothers' designs were strongly in tune with the movement's basic design tenets, their creative scope expanded to include a large number of Japanese touches after they visited the World's Columbian Exposition in Chicago in 1893.

Japan's Ho-o-den pavilion at the Chicago exposition was one of the fair's most popular exhibits, and the Greene brothers, no different from anyone else, entered the simple structure with great anticipation. The clean, uncluttered interior, bathed in soft, soothing colors, possessed a serene charm unlike anything they had ever seen. Realizing that the Japanese and the Arts and Crafts architectural styles complemented one another beautifully, they traveled on to California, where they would apply much of what they had seen in the Ho-o-den pavilion to their work. With rustic shingles, healthful sleeping porches, and low, overhanging eaves derived from Oriental examples, their homes fit extraordinarily well into the California landscape. After touring America and visiting the Greenes, the British designer Charles Ashbee wrote in 1909: "Like Frank Lloyd Wright the spell of Japan is upon them. They feel the beauty and make magic out of the horizontal line."

The highly original and often emulated architect Frank Lloyd Wright built the Hollyhock House in Hollywood in 1920 for the oil heiress Aline Barnsdall. In this house Wright combined the elegant, understated elements for which he was famous, with touches of whimsy throughout; his high-backed chairs, flower-shaped columns, Japanese screens, and art-glass windows ingeniously tied the outdoors to the indoors. Wright felt that "the ideal dining room is a bright, cozy, cheerful place you involuntarily enter with a smile" and filled his dining spaces with soothing yellows, golds, ochers, reds, and greens that created a warm yet stimulating environment conducive to memorable dining and good conversation. His 1923 Storer House in Los Angeles, with its rugged concrete building blocks, seems to grow out of the arid Western earth like a huge cactus, with the surrounding hills seen from every conceivable angle through dozens of windows.

While California was particularly well suited for Arts and Crafts architecture, Americans from all over the country were drawn to the

**OPPOSITE:** *Intricate examples of Aesthetic bronze or bronze-and-silver metalworking craftsmanship. A Tiffany & Co. spoon, Gorham's fruit knife and fork with an 1890 design of birds and bamboo, an 1882 Gorham tea caddy, a cigarette case by Gorham, a small tray, and a small scent bottle fashioned in silver and bronze—all reflect the influence of Aesthetic Movement Orientalism spanning the 1880–1910 period.*

**ABOVE:** *An Oriental mood is evident in these Martelé silver pieces made by Gorham during the 1890s. Included are a pair of sugar tongs, copper tongs with a metallic patina, and a cream and sugar set. Dominick and Haff, Inc., fashioned the turn-of-the-century salt dish, mustard pot, and butter plate.*

charms of the style; one of its most notable supporters, George Gough Booth, publisher of the *Detroit Evening News,* supported Arts and Crafts artists and designers by turning his home, Cranbrook House, into an educational complex. Booth commissioned such noted designers as Arthur J. Stone, Elizabeth Copeland, and Omar Ramsden to embellish the house, and students from all across America came to Cranbrook to study. Booth's dedication to the style, much like Samuel Bing's to Art Nouveau, helped make it accessible to Americans as tablewares made by top designers were introduced into many of the large department stores.

The Arts and Crafts Movement eventually became much more than just a style; it would be, for many, a way of life that touched every facet of daily existence. Rooms flowed into one another, gratuitous ornamentation was frowned upon, objects were made to be pleasing to the touch, and there was an intense interest in landscaping and garden design. The founding of the Arts and Crafts Exhibition Society in England in 1887 provided an outlet where the public could see the work of the leading practitioners of the movement, perhaps even attend a lecture by the great William Morris himself on the movement's underlying principles, and, of course, buy a thing or two. Morris's suggestion to "have nothing in your house that you do not know to be useful or believe to be beautiful" must be credited with encouraging artisans to do some of their finest work.

The movement's design tenets echoed throughout the decorative arts, inspiring glassmakers and silversmiths to return to the basics: stained and hand-blown glass and hand-hammered metalwork enjoyed a renaissance, while potters returned to the wheel to create one-of-a-kind vases and tiles that featured hand-sculpted botanical relief and subtle matte glazes. William Morris was the philosophical leader of the movement, and his contribution to each of the style's decorative arts was im-

**OPPOSITE:** *An orchid is beautifully displayed in a handsome 1904 copper-and-wood centerpiece with amber glass shades designed by Frank Lloyd Wright.*

**ABOVE:** *This Tiffany gilt-bronze candelabra is a handsome work of art.*

Illuminating the Arts and Crafts style of the major international silversmiths, a Tiffany silver candelabra from 1920 brings to life the figures in a Herter Looms tapestry. **OPPOSITE, ABOVE LEFT:** an Arts and Crafts trio displayed before a Flemish tapestry includes a Venetian blue-stem champagne glass, a Georg Jensen candelabra, and a covered bowl with an enamel finial by Omar Ramsden; **ABOVE RIGHT:** an intricately carved wood panel at Cranbrook House shows off a marvelous Georg Jensen double-arm candlestick with grape clusters and lilies of the valley. **BELOW LEFT:** A 1903–1910 Wiener Werkstätte piece that is reminiscent of Josef Hoffmann's work; **BELOW RIGHT:** this candelabra shows Arthur Stone's fondness for grape clusters and foliate etching.

measurable—he designed textiles, porcelain, glass, silver, wallpapers, and furniture and marketed his goods through Liberty & Company in London, thus creating a prominent showcase for his own and fellow artisans' work. His abstract leafy and nature-inspired patterns are almost as popular today as they were in the nineteenth century. Royal Doulton produced china that was directly related to Morris's designs and color choices, as did Tiffany, who used Moorish patterns as inspiration for some of his work. The beauty of the china made during the Arts and Crafts period is in its subdued patterning, which allows us today to mix it with contemporary pieces without fear of clashing; also its predominantly subtle colors work well with today's tableware, giving us many opportunities to set tables that combine the best of the old with the new.

The opening up of Japan to the West by Admiral Perry in 1853–1854, after centuries of isolation, gave Europeans and Americans a rich new source for design inspiration. During the 1880s, almost every maker of china registered a "Japanese" design with the Patent Office. The essential element in all of these designs was an asymmetrical arrangement of fans, birds, or sunflowers within the framework of the circular plate. The practice of running a band of design diagonally across the face of the plate or

**OPPOSITE:** *This extraordinary enamel and silver box made by talented Arts and Crafts artisan Elizabeth Copeland in 1922 is set upon a Gothic Revival chair.*

**BELOW:** *Inspired perhaps by an illuminated manuscript like the one in the photograph, this Austrian monogrammed filigree-glass dessert plate was made as a gift for the fiftieth wedding anniversary of the Booths, owners of Cranbrook House.*

cutting up the entire pattern with a series of bands was also popular, particularly with Wedgwood, which made a complete service called Sparrow and Bamboo that combined relief molding with transfer printing.

Art pottery was a relatively inexpensive way for American consumers to fill their homes with art, and a huge market for handcrafted ceramics, including California's Catalina pottery, was born. Stylistically, there were basically two categories of American art pottery: wares emphasizing form and glaze, and those emphasizing applied decoration. Arts and Crafts ceramics were specifically made to complement the style's architecture and furniture; to this end, realistic depictions of plants and flowers were replaced by more abstract, simplified forms. The housing boom of the 1880s and 1890s in America led to an increased demand for ceramic tiles, which appealed because they were easy to keep clean and brought an artistic dash to the kitchen, bathroom, fireplace surround, or entrance hall of suburban homes. In America, at least fifty tile companies were founded between 1875 and 1920, producing molded, glazed tiles with Japanese-inspired designs of birds, fans, and small geometric patterns.

The Arts and Crafts silver industry heeded the call to return to hand-craftsmanship, and even the largest manufacturers, like Gorham, set up smaller studios specifically for such time-honored silver-making techniques as hammering and hand chasing. Stroke marks were proudly left on the metal's surface as proof of its maker's hand in Gorham's stunningly successful line called Martelé. Combining elements of both the Art Nouveau and the Arts and Crafts styles, Martelé featured countless Japanese details, such as egrets, fans, bamboo stalks, and lotus blossoms. Today, such richly decorated silver can be used for a special dinner party or be interspersed with new pieces for a Sunday brunch or luncheon.

Tiffany & Co. often combined silver and copper, with silver inlay

picking out designs on painted copper surfaces; popular designs on coffee sets and candlesticks incorporated such Japanese motifs as Oriental flowers, vines, gourds, fish, and dragonflies. Tiffany's also was influenced by American Indian design, and exhibited a silver bowl with copper-and-niello inlay at the 1893 World's Columbian Exposition in Chicago; the bowl exhibited by the company resembled, in shape, a Pueblo Indian basket, and Tiffany's would continue tapping into the Native American heritage for many years to come.

Arthur J. Stone, an Englishman by birth, moved to America and became one of its finest silversmiths working in the Arts and Crafts tradition. Stone wore a gray smock while he worked, signifying the silversmith's trade, and embellished his work with flower details applied with a delicate hand; his elegant work is reminiscent of embroidery done with spun silver instead of with thread. A superb craftsman, Stone also captured nature's fragile beauty in his work, decorating much of his flatware, as well as his bowls, coffee sets, and candlesticks with botanical motifs.

England's Charles Robert Ashbee was enthralled by Ruskin's writings and became an ardent follower of the Arts and Crafts

Movement; he established his own guild, where he produced silver tableware featuring peacocks, ships, the sun, the tree of life, and the pink, the beloved English flower. Ashbee's silver was filled with finely drawn wires and carefully raised domes; his decorations reflected more of an appreciation of folk art than of functionalism.

The work of Omar Ramsden, who was also English, was highly individualistic with its virtuoso use of the hammer-mark finish. Ramsden's more important commissions were usually in a Tudor style that featured repoussé ornament of roses and galleons; his later work was distinctly indebted to the graphic art of Hans Holbein.

The Arts and Crafts Movement provided a wealth of subjects for glassmakers—particularly for William Morris, who worked in stained glass; medieval heroes and heroines abounded, astride regal white horses adorned with jeweled harnesses and saddles. Architects, such as Frank Lloyd Wright, Charles Rennie Mackintosh, and Charles and Henry Greene, liked to embellish their houses with stained-glass panels of their own design: the Greenes' famous Gamble House in Pasadena, California, features a magnificent widespreading tree in stained glass for the front entrance; Frank Lloyd Wright preferred flat, geometric designs that he felt didn't detract from the natural view of the landscape beyond. The same rich, warm colors that were used in stained-glass windows showed up in table glass of the period, and are particularly appealing today as we move more and more toward a natural style of decorating for our homes and our tables.

Some of Steuben's glassware lines had evocative names that conjured up images of distant lands and eras: Millefiori was named after ancient mosaic glass; the etched Intarsia and crackled Moss Agate, the translucent Mandarin Yellow, Aurene, and Verre de Soie were inspired by ancient Chinese porcelain. In keeping with the interest in nature and

**ABOVE:** *A turn-of-the-century German coffee set in Moorish style blends modern shapes with the hand-wrought texture of Martelé silver.*

Japanese motifs, many glassmakers, such as Koloman Moser in Austria, created stemware and candelabra that featured clusters of fruit and flowers applied to simple shapes, often in colors like yellow or grape.

The mellow, handcrafted style of the Arts and Crafts Movement soon became a victim of the rage for Modernism in the early 1920s, but fortunately its beauty was rediscovered after languishing for almost five decades. In the early 1970s, an exhibition titled "The Arts and Crafts Movement in America: 1876–1916" was held at Princeton University, and eventually traveled to Chicago and to Washington, D.C. Soon after the "California Design, 1910" exhibition at the Pasadena Art Center, also staged in the 1970s, Tiffany's reissued several of its Arts and Crafts patterns, including the Frank Lloyd Wright china patterns designed for Japan's Imperial Hotel in 1922.

As we find ourselves in the midst of our own revolution—not an industrial one, but certainly a communications revolution—Americans are once again strongly drawn to the same movement that so appealed to them almost one hundred years ago. Surely the relaxing quality of the style and its early hints of today's minimalism are reasons for its current surge of popularity. Arts and Crafts houses are like refuges in a storm; they embrace and nurture, soothe and refresh—something we all need after a long day navigating our way through the Internet. Although very few of us can live in the wonderful houses built by the great icons of the movement, like the Greene brothers and Frank Lloyd Wright, we all can recapture some of the personality of the period by incorporating pieces of Arts and Crafts china, silver, and glass into our modern tablescapes.

The tablewares made in the less-is-more approach to design that was synonymous with the Arts and Crafts style blend in very well on contemporary tables and grace one's home with a welcome touch of the high moral principles, integrity, and rich aesthetic of one of the century's most purposeful movements.

**ABOVE:** *A Greene and Greene lamp decorated with a silhouetted landscape illuminates Coalport's cobalt-and-gold plate decorated with birds and bamboo.*

**OPPOSITE:** *A dragonfly vase by Christofle and a Tiffany butterfly lamp sit on a library table in the Gamble House designed by Greene and Greene.*

# Beaux-Arts & Revivalism

While the proponents of the more progressive Arts and Crafts and Art Nouveau movements generated a great deal of excitement and notoriety in a relatively small segment of the population drawn to avant-garde styles, their call for radical change was not answered by the great majority, who found comfort in the familiarity that makes most of us return to the more traditional, classic designs of the past, recalling a time when life seemed more manageable and people seemed more civilized.

In the world of art and design the fascination with yesterday ebbs and flows with the tide of current taste. Today, as Jane Austen and other classic authors top the best-seller lists, and the stages of Broadway host an inordinate number of revivals, we

**PRECEDING PAGES:** *Dining* en plein air *in a classic garden alleé-and-fountain landscape setting on the grounds of a Beaux-Arts mansion calls for an imaginative mix of traditional tablewares. Belgian Art Nouveau glass by Val St. Lambert and Copeland 1890s plates of swirled gold with a twig-and-rose border share a skirted table with Lombardy fluted and scalloped plates by Royal Crown Derby and a 1920 cake dish by Coalport. Flora Danica botanical-handle flatware and a Meissen pot de crème set are included. Dresden porcelain place cards add a personal touch.*

**ABOVE AND RIGHT:** *A late 1800s French cut-crystal chandelier is suspended above a unique glass-topped table with a base composed of a trio of cavorting dolphins in an elegant conservatory overlooking the gardens. Royal Swansea and Haviland china, thumbprint glasses, Bimini 1925 candlesticks, blown-glass figurals, and 1920s Frigast hammered silver are on the table.*

seem to be particularly enraptured by the past, and yet there are always those restless souls among us who break free and fearlessly soar into the future.

At the turn of the last century, a particularly keen interest in the classic style took hold, encouraged by writers like Edith Wharton and Henry James (who thought America so uncouth, he relinquished his citizenship); Mrs. Wharton and Elsie de Wolfe, who called herself America's first female interior decorator, encouraged a return to the elegance of some of history's most beautiful decorative styles. Both James and Wharton had visited Charles Eliot Norton of Harvard University, one of New England's great intellectuals, and his daughter, Sara, at his summer home in Ashfield, Massachusetts, where they discussed world events and the ideas of Ruskin, who was a friend of Norton's. The days spent with the Nortons imbued Edith Wharton with an interest in the new philosophies being advocated in the design world; although holding fast to classical design, she was blessed with an open mind and drew inspiration from such discussions. Bernard Berenson, the great art historian, also studied under Charles Eliot Norton—a fact that points to the important flow of ideas among writers, educators, and artists at this time.

The reform movements that grew out of the rejection of what was considered the vulgarity of modernism appealed to many like-minded thinkers, who willingly agreed to turn the clock back—for some, the retreat from the present led all the way back to ancient times. In America, interest in Pilgrim furniture as well as the civilizations of ancient Greece and Rome had been kindled at the 1876 Centennial Exposition in Philadelphia, where the decorative arts on display featured designs closely linking the practical and artistic achievements of Americans with those of great historical figures.

**ABOVE:** *Christofle Malmaison silver, jade green twirled glasses with funnel stems, and Limoges china with a gilded fresco design evoke a Tuscan mood.*

**ABOVE:** *Handsome ivory-handled utensils serve the salad, and Art Nouveau etched glasses with faceted stems hold the wine.*

**RIGHT:** *An Italianate buffet is set up in the pool house at the Virginia Robinson gardens.*

Americans rigorously tried to resurrect the classical age, and artisans of tablewares responded to the rage for historically correct decorative objects made in a strict Beaux-Arts tradition.

The Beaux-Arts style was a vein of late-nineteenth-century classicism based on the teaching at the influential École des Beaux-Arts in Paris, which had replaced, in the early eighteenth century, the former royal schools of painting, sculpture, and architecture. The school adopted a rigidly taught curriculum that included measuring, drawing, and paper reconstructions of noted ancient Roman monuments, particularly the Pantheon.

A large number of American students went to Paris to study the Beaux-Arts doctrine, most likely driven by a desire to soak up some European culture that they could bring back with them to their less sophisticated homeland. For those Americans who could not afford to venture abroad, a generous sampling of the very best of Beaux-Arts design could be found at home.

Once again, we return to Chicago's 1893 World's Columbian Exposition. Almost everyone who visited it stopped first at the raucous Midway Plaisance, a mile-long strip of rides, sideshows, and concession booths that served up everything from belly dancers in the Little Egypt Theater to a 250-foot Ferris wheel. From the Midway, a short jaunt under a little bridge would bring fairgoers to The White City—the exposition's magnificent alabaster Beaux-Arts exhibition halls.

Within the walls of The White City, a dazzling collection of the finest tableware of the day was displayed, including two monumental pieces by

**ABOVE:** *A 1910 tea and coffee service with wood handles is a fine example of classic Beaux-Arts design with graceful swag and garland embossing. The finials on the teapot and coffee pot are in the form of pineapples, the symbol of hospitality,*

Tiffany & Co. that masterfully blended classical and exotic motifs. George W. Shiebler exhibited his Homeric pattern medallion flatware, decorated with sculpted portraits of ancient Greek figures, such as Achilles and Hercules, based on images in pattern books of ancient sculpture. The massive exhibit dedicated to academic tradition was so impressive, it led to the formation of The Society of Beaux-Arts Architects in New York in 1895, which would eventually become the Beaux-Arts Institute of Design in 1911.

As the United States became involved in World War I, it became increasingly clear that relations with many of the countries from which America had imported china would probably never be the same, and American china companies responded to this reality by stepping up all facets of their operations. Soon after 1918, the American Bureau of Education issued a pamphlet maintaining the importance of industrial-art training in improving the quality of American goods. The American Association of Museums, citing the fact that the Victoria and Albert Museum in London regularly provided historical information to decorative artists and manufacturers for use in their work, suggested that American museums develop divisions to do what the British had been doing for years; this increased emphasis on museum collections also contributed to the proliferation of ceramics strongly influenced by the past.

The period that fostered the so-called reform movements, such as Arts and Crafts, Beaux-Arts classicism, and the multitude of revivals was a time of great wealth. The heady affluence and heightened confidence of the in-

**OPPOSITE, ABOVE:** *Set for a quiet dinner in the library of the Robinson House, there are a 1915 Dresden gilt-and-cobalt dessert plate with fruit urns, a large 1910 square charger by Minton, and Whiting Lily pattern silver on an Italianate marquetry folding table done in the Louis XV style.*

**BELOW:** *It is time for tea at the Robinson House. Capidomonte cups and saucers are set on an English Sheraton table with Mrs. Robinson's silver tea service.*

dustrial age not only produced fine home furnishings; it also created an unprecedented number of American millionaires. The increase in the number of people who could afford to travel or take the Grand Tour of Europe and beyond created a surge of interest in exotic cultures. This fascination was reflected in the choices of patterns used in all of the decorative arts of the period, and tables set during this time were particularly rich in motifs borrowed from all around the globe.

By the years 1910 to 1919, decorating books and home-decorating magazines were advocating homes filled with copies of earlier-style furniture, fabrics, rugs, pictures, silver, glass, and porcelain, in a sincere effort to reform the decorative arts, which, they felt, had deteriorated in both quality and high aesthetic purpose. Although this era more or less coincided with the beginnings of antiques collecting on a widespread basis in America, most Americans relied on reproductions, which were highly valued and not looked down upon for not being antiques; in fact, at many of the period's fairs and exhibitions, newly made furniture and decorative objects were displayed proudly alongside the genuine thing to illustrate the degree to which the artist had meticulously copied the original.

Furniture manufacturers across America, including Wallace Nutting, who accurately predicted that one day furniture bearing his name would be coveted by collectors, crafted pieces in a wide assortment of historical styles to please the public; Nutting asserted in 1930, "There is enshrined in the forms of furniture used by our ancestors a spirit absent from the exotic shapes that came from Italy and France."

The Colonial Revival style appealed to many Americans as they struggled to adopt a national style that they felt accurately captured their nation's heritage. A popular journalist at the time put it this way: "Let American manufacturers make their own designs and leave off copying foreign ones!" Colonial Revival ranged from faithful reproductions to broader renditions of Queen Anne, Georgian, Adam, and Sheraton styles

**OPPOSITE:** *Coffee in the library of the Ford House is set on a seventeenth-century refectory table on top of which sits a sixteenth-century Ming Dynasty vase that has been made into a lamp. Minton 1920s gilded jade-green and bone-white demitasse cups are accompanied by a Martelé silver coffee pot.*

**ABOVE:** *Delicate Venetian gold-filigree, hand-blown champagne glasses.*

**OPPOSITE, ABOVE:** *Gold-wash ice cream server and spoons by Gorham in the Palm pattern and a Tiffany Art Nouveau cucumber server.*

**OPPOSITE, below:** *Gold-wash berry spoons and a silver Arts and Crafts dish.*

and was at its peak between 1910 and 1925, although it remains quite popular to this day.

Always eager to increase sales, silverware manufacturers added hollowware and flatware patterns in the Colonial Revival style to their production lines in the late 1880s; there was a small historical exhibit of early American silverware at the 1893 World's Columbian Exposition in Chicago, and soon after that, the first major exhibition of American silver was held at the Museum of Fine Arts in Boston, followed by three others organized by New York's Metropolitan Museum of Art in 1907, 1909, and 1911.

Despite the renewed interest in Colonial designs, it is important to note that the bread-and-butter business of the silver, as well as the china and glass companies, was neoclassical designs, which accounted for most of what people chose for their tables. Today, the wealth of the pieces produced in these traditional patterns makes it possible for the contemporary host to arrange tables in a classic mood that is timelessly elegant.

Silver makers incorporated key motifs of the Colonial, Federal, Rococo, and Grecian styles, such as festoons, garlands, swags, floral and fruit decorations, ribbons, putti, classical urns, and ovals in their wares during this period and on into the 1930s. Gorham's flatware patterns Brookdale, Buttercup, Douglas, Fleury, Paris, Poppy, Marguerite, Montclair, Tuileries, and many others relied on pretty floral motifs captured on swags and garlands that cascaded completely down the handles. In addition, Gorham made candelabra, bowls, and vases that carefully encompassed seventeenth-, eighteenth-, and nineteenth-century English and French silver designs; in particular, the silver service patterns of silversmith F. Antoine Heller, who came from Paris to work for Gorham in

1881, were crisp and minutely detailed in pure Beaux-Arts tradition. Also, Towle, Whiting, Reed and Barton, and Tiffany catered to the taste for Revival styles as well. In England, in 1903, many flatware sets, particularly fish and dessert services with mother-of-pearl or ivory handles, were made to please Edwardian tastes.

As the rage for historicism grew, glass companies responded to the demand for period pieces by reviving a number of past styles using etched, molded, and cut glass. Cut glass continued to enjoy the popularity it had in the 1890s well into the twentieth century, and housewives were reminded by various magazines such as *House Beautiful,* that cut glass was the "most showy, and in many respects, choicest of table equipments."

Libbey Glass of Toledo, Ohio, attracted the eye of the public with its ruby-colored glass, first shown at its miniature plant open to the public at the Chicago exposition. There Libbey produced a large number of pattern-glass pieces, especially tumblers and small creamers that were flashed with color. Seneca, Morgantown, Lotus,

**OPPOSITE:** *These grape-color-cut-to-clear Moser glasses, circa 1937, are part of a large service that belonged to the Booth family. The 1918 silver compote with grape clusters was made by Georg Jensen in Denmark, and it illustrates the compatibility of fine design from one era or style to another.* **ABOVE:** *A Minton 1910–1920 enameled dinner plate with a flower urn and a cornucopia design emulates the fruit-filled urns in the stained-glass window at Van Dyke Place.*

Franciscan, and Cambridge all produced glassware in Revival styles, as did Tiffin, which produced cut, colored, and etched stemware beautifully decorated with such motifs as ribbons and garlands, laurel leaves, urns, cupids, exotic and game birds, and flower-filled baskets that closely identified the many different Revival styles. Glass manufacturers wisely used pattern names that conveyed the style each line attempted to reproduce. Adams, Apollo, Athens, Classic, Diana, Dolley Madison, Empire, Grecian Star, Jefferson, Monticello, and Regency give some indication of the vast selection of Revival styles offered.

Fostoria specialized in Colonial Revival pressed glass between 1901 and 1925, creating patterns like Bedford, Essex, and Puritan, which featured long, plain panels or simple, broad flutes. Their American pattern, with its simple, elegant arrangement of small cubes, became quite famous, and for decades pieces of American were considered to be perfect gifts for a newly married couple. Heisey's refined Plain Band and Touraine and their gold-banded glassware patterns were also highly sought after as wedding presents; many brides of the 1920s and their children or grandchildren still cherish these pieces today.

The Wall Street crash of 1929 heralded the Great Depression, when people were lucky if they had enough money to get by, let alone to spend on luxury items. In response to the dismal economic climate in America, glass companies produced lines that could be purchased with little money and yet, with their attractive designs and uplifting colors, brought a much-needed jolt of beauty into even the bleakest of hard times. While such glass was usually sold in five-and-dime stores like Woolworth or Kresge, it was also often included as a gift in boxes of cereal or laundry detergent or with the purchase of a few gallons of gas. The glassware that sprang from these humble beginnings would one day be massed under the general label Depression Glass and be highly sought after by collectors for its color and rich assortment of pleasing patterns. Green, amber, pink, and deep blue were favorite colors for Depression Glass, but ruby-

**OPPOSITE:** *Attesting to the delicacy, variety, and beauty of elegant colored stemware, this collection of yellow etched glasses is set upon an 1850 gold-and-black papier-mâché tray at Meadow Brook Hall. Fostoria's June, Cashmere, Trojan, and Versailles patterns, and Tiffin's Le Fleur, Flanders, and Caneva patterns are just a smattering of innovative designs from the 1920s to 1930s that are prized today.*

red, pale blue, and soft peach were also used, as well as clear glass lavishly decorated with pattern. Often, two colors were used—one for the stem of the glass, with another used for the body; pink and green were an especially pretty and popular combination.

Cambridge, Anchor-Hocking, Fostoria, A. H. Heisey & Company, Fenton, U.S. Glass, Paden City, McKee, Imperial, and Hazel-Atlas glass companies were the largest American manufacturers specializing in the production of Depression Glass, producing many lines of tableware as well as kitchenware items like mixing bowls, salt and pepper shakers, canisters, even hair-tonic bottles. Tiffin Glass made a black, satin-finish line for tableware and dresser sets that was a popular seller during the thirties, while in 1940 it introduced a variety of new shades that departed from the more traditional Depression-era colors: Banana (bright yellow), Killarney (emerald-green), Plum (deep purple), and Copen Blue (ice-blue). Today, what would be lovelier than a luncheon table set with Depression-era glasses of pink and green, maybe set off with a centerpiece of complementary roses? The mix-and-match possibilities are endless, and Depression Glass still remains well priced, making it particularly attractive to young couples and those just beginning on what will undoubtedly turn out to be a lifelong love of collecting vintage glass.

In the major ceramics factories in England, a number of extremely talented artists were employed to hand-paint china with pastoral and

**ABOVE:** *A gold-and-silver-overlay dinner plate, part of a Bavarian service from the 1920s that was a favorite of Anna Thompson Dodge, who often used it for major dinners.*

**OPPOSITE:** *1920s silver-overlay serving plates, displayed as art on a marble mantel at the Robinson House, echo the elegance of a Venetian mirror.*

neoclassical scenes and themes. At Minton, Antonin Boullemier specialized in painting small children and cupids; Royal Worcester's John and Harry Stinton painted Highland cattle studies that captured the pastoral ambience of Olde England; and Richard Sebright's forte was flowers and copies of famous Old Masters paintings. Harry Davis, also of Royal Worcester, copied paintings by Corot and did some marvelous landscapes and city scenes. In 1922, Worcester produced tea and coffee services with neoclassic Adam-style borders. Minton deftly blended Adam-revival garlands and Edwardian medallions into its tableware, as well as Rococo shapes with Oriental motifs, and classical shapes with medieval designs; often, Minton used raised gilding against a popular shade of blue called Bleu Celeste.

Although American china companies, such as Lenox China, which had been established in New Jersey in 1889, still emulated foreign designs and even proclaimed, as Sebring Pottery did in 1901, that their work was "A dead ringer for French china!" more and more companies proudly produced dinnerware with names like American Beauty, Arlington, Dolley Madison, Mayflower, Mount Vernon, Plymouth, Saint Louis, and Martha Washington, which were contemporary versions of early American designs and patterns. American companies also made dinnerware sets in Louis XIV, Louis XVI, Rococo, and Adam styles, although they took an understandable delight in coming up with lines like American Girl, which sought to capture the wholesome beauty and charm of young American women who were finally edging away from the standards of European beauty. The magnificence of the American landscape was alluded to in lines such as America, Hudson, Nevada, and Niagara.

The newly rich built America's largest and grandest residences and hotels; dozens of rooms called for decorating on a

grandiose scale, and European castles and stately homes often served as decorating primers for the nouveau riche faced with the daunting challenge of embellishing their huge estates. Why, then, did so many of America's greatest financial titans choose reproductions for their American manor homes? It was, most likely, due to a new pride in machine-made American goods, coupled with a desire for the opulent look of European furniture, tableware, and decorative accessories. A combination of traditional American eighteenth-century styles with an updated twentieth-century outlook and a smattering of English or Continental styling seemed to please even the fussiest captain of industry.

No expense was spared as Detroit's automobile barons built homes for their families in the city where their fortunes were made; out west in California, successful entrepreneurs hired great architects to design their estates. Edsel and Eleanor Ford's Cotswold-style mansion, Matilda Dodge Wilson's one-hundred-room Meadow Brook Hall, Anna Thompson Dodge's estate Rosecliff—perhaps the most elegant and refined Beaux-Arts mansion ever built in America, which unfortunately stood only for thirty short years before becoming a victim of the wrecking ball in the 1970s, Detroit's Van Dyke house, and California's Robinson house all sprang to life during the peak of America's love of historical revivals, and their architectural lines and eclectically furnished interiors reflect the tastes of the time. The women who ran these magnificent homes

**OPPOSITE:** *In the Presidential Suite of The Greenbrier, an eclectic mix of Minton's typical 1910–1930s china designs with Edwardian medallions and swags complement an interplay of glasswares. Cambridge clear-etched Diana, Fostoria's pink-etched Navarre, and green-stemmed wines would enhance any table setting today.*

**LEFT:** *America's own Gibson Girl is immortalized on a series of amusing plates by Royal Doulton, perhaps alluding to the desire of American heiresses to marry British titles. They show her daily round of activities, including a formal dinner party.*

were forerunners of today's hostesses, who practice mixing and matching tableware from a variety of periods. Although the earlier woman had a huge treasure trove of tableware from which to choose,

those of us with an artistic eye and even a modest number of pretty patterns from which to choose can successfully emulate the beautiful tables those gracious hostesses set.

After visiting castles and manor houses in England, Matilda Dodge, who married the lumber baron Alfred Wilson, after her husband John's death in 1920, commissioned the architect William E. Kapp to build Meadow Brook Hall in the style of a great Tudor manor house in England. Despite the home's distinctly English character, she took great pains to decorate it with many American-made goods in keeping

with the newfound pride of Americans in the quality of "homegrown" products. Beautifully designed stained-glass windows were created for a number of rooms, including a set picturing hunting and culinary scenes for the dining room. A delightful touch in the ballroom is the juxtaposition, in stone, of two "jesters"—one is a medieval one hard at work trying to make the king laugh in his court, whereas the other one is America's beloved Charlie Chaplin.

Also in the 1920s, the Edsel Fords engaged one of America's finest architects, Albert Kahn, to design and build their home, a glorious sixty-room, cozy, ivy-covered Cotswold "cottage," which they filled with the finest European furnishings, and a large number of paintings by such artists as Matisse, Cézanne, and Raphael. There is a surprise in the wood-

**OPPOSITE AND ABOVE:**
*The Pink Room at The Whitney, a confection of elaborate Beaux-Arts detailing, set aglow with soft lighting and a collection of tinted glass set on a Chantilly lace cloth. Dessert is served in Venetian champagne flutes. The table is set with pink cut-to-clear Venetian glass, pink floral-cartouche dinner plates by Cauldon used as oversized dessert plates. A three-tier silver and cut-glass dessert stand is used to display a miniature garden of pink impatiens.*

paneled, very traditional house—the appropriately named Modern Room, designed in the 1930s by Walter Dorwin Teague, one of America's leading industrial designers in the Art Deco style— which will be discussed in detail in the next chapter. The inclusion of this room in the house, as well as a number of other, similar rooms designed for the Dodge children, strongly illustrates the split personality of a time when the comfort of the past was pitted against the unfamiliarity of the new.

The Greenbrier Hotel of White Sulphur Springs, West Virginia, has been the place to dance, swim, take the waters, and relax in the sun ever since the railroad boom of the post–Civil War era made the resort accessible for both wealthy and middle-class visitors from all over the country. People came to The Greenbrier to experience all of its recreational facilities (although more than a few young men probably came with high hopes of seeing a genuine Southern belle, Irene Langhorne, who was the model for Charles Dana Gibson's Gibson Girl drawings). The Greenbrier and all the remarkable homes mentioned above serve as perfectly harmonious backdrops for many of the table settings in this book; in later chapters, we will explore how the residents of these historically rich residences might have lived and entertained; perhaps they can teach us a thing or two about what it means to live the good life and what it takes to create table settings that will be remembered and talked about long after the last dish is cleared.

The wave of historicism that swept across the decorative arts in the early part of the twentieth century eventually receded as modern influences flooded the studios of silver, glass, and china makers. It became increasingly difficult for the buying public to turn away from the exciting work being done in startlingly streamlined designs that echoed the fast pace of a dynamic era. Young people, dazzled by images in magazines and newspapers, and especially on Hollywood's silver screen, gradually were won over by the eye-popping style called Art Deco.

**OPPOSITE:** *A magnificent classic centerpiece showing the Three Graces holding garlands is part of Cranbrook's renowned silver collection.*

# ART DECO

Zigzags and ziggurats, skyscrapers, streamline and jazz—these words are filled with a raw kinetic energy that makes just reading them prompt the heart to beat a little faster. Each one of them manages to capture in a flash the exuberance of l'Art Déco, or Art Deco, the decorative style that prevailed throughout Europe and America between the Paris exposition of 1925 and the outbreak of World War II.

Art Deco's spirit encompassed the moods of three decades: the 1920s, when blue-blooded denizens of society could be spotted doing the Charleston, sipping bathtub gin from teacups, and swallowing goldfish on a dare; the 1930s, when even the grimness of the Great Depression couldn't squelch the upbeat, sensuous rhythms of swing or keep young women from plucking

their eyebrows and bleaching their marcelled waves platinum blond like Jean Harlow's; and the early 1940s, when romantic Hollywood movies offered a comforting respite from wartime realities, young men strutted down the streets in zoot suits, and Frank Sinatra's singing made young girls in bobby sox and saddle shoes swoon.

Whereas the Arts and Crafts Movement had elevated the art of the handcrafted, Art Deco emphasized the machine's artistic possibilities in the manufacture of china, glass, and silver tableware. The shiny, spare lines of the industrial age were roundly applauded, not derided as they had been before; superfluous decoration was rejected in favor of angular, unadorned forms, with the inherent quality of the material used conspicuously accentuated. Japonisme, Symbolism, Historicism, Arts and Crafts, and Art Nouveau were all challenged as a widespread search for a new, more modern style began.

The Art Deco style began to coalesce as early as 1910, when the architects Erich Mendelssohn and Eliel Saarinen first began to work out streamlined building designs, which would eventually lead to the design principles used in such landmarks as the Chrysler and Empire State buildings, Golden Gate Bridge, and Radio City Music Hall. The Bauhaus in Germany and Austria's Wiener Werkstätte, as well as such art movements as Cubism, Expressionism, Futurism, and Fauvism, and a growing awareness of African art, contributed vital design elements to the movement and the style. The 1925 Exposition Internationale des Arts Décoratifs et Industriels Modernes was an event that marked a turning point in the international design world—the free-flowing lines of Art

Nouveau gave way to a pure geometry that was sparse and clean yet filled with decorative fillips that borrowed from such diverse sources as sacred objects discovered in Tutankhamen's tomb in 1922; futuristic images drawn from Buck Rogers's world; and twentieth-century visions of high-speed trains, planes, and automobiles.

Although the ceramics, glass, silver, furniture, and textiles displayed at the 1925 Paris exposition were decorated with somewhat traditional and romantic motifs, such as closely gathered flowers in garlands and baskets, stylized rosebuds, doves, prancing deer, fountains, tassels, and tightly wound ropes of pearls, by the late 1920s and early 1930s the designs had become noticeably more geometric, more in line with what most people today consider Art Deco. By the 1940s a racy streamlined appearance, echoing the new high-speed trains, was a premier element in decorative arts; it sometimes led to objects that looked humorously fu-

**BELOW:** *A Pickard gold teapot, sugar, and creamer sit beside a bronze sculpture by Carl Milles at Saarinen House.*

turistic and space age. It is best to view Art Deco as a fascinating blend of design moods that changed over the 1920s, 1930s, and 1940s rather than as a fixed style that can be easily pigeonholed; it is this chameleon-like quality that, for many, makes Art Deco a fascinating visual history of three decades.

By 1930, virtually all facets of American design were steeped in glamorous Art Deco style: supermarkets, gas stations, drive-in hamburger stands, diners, the interiors of railway stations and hotels, department stores like New York's Bloomingdale's and California's Bullock's Wilshire, hair dryers, toasters, even vacuum cleaners adopted sleek, modernistic forms. The luxury transatlantic ocean liner *Queen Mary,* which first set sail in 1936, was fully outfitted in high Deco style, with each departure from port made with no less than 100,000 pieces of china and 21,000 tablecloths at the ready.

Art Deco's charm was warmly embraced in America by design-

**OPPOSITE:** *For a golden dinner at Saarinen House, Pickard china, Orrefors and Tiffin glass, and early Bakelite knives and forks are set upon a round Eliel Saarinen table that radiates like the sun and can easily be made smaller for intimate dinners.*

**ABOVE, LEFT:** *This 1928 coffee service of globular design by Bertoia has elongated finials.*

**ABOVE, RIGHT:** *This unusual round Peoplé placemat was designed by Loja Saarinen, Eliel's daughter.*

**ABOVE:** *Concentric circles form a sleek Art Deco motif in this Wiener Werkstätte tea trio.*

**OPPOSITE, ABOVE:** *Set on a table in the liner museum* Queen Mary *are Frank Lloyd Wright china, a silver-rimmed martini glass from 1930, a Christofle silver tray, candelabra, and their America flatware pattern.*

**OPPOSITE, BELOW:** *Heinrich and Company china hits the mark with pure Deco design that features concentric circles and silver overlay that echo the stylish metal fire-screen design.*

ers, both decorative and industrial, and the style subsequently played a large role in Chicago's 1933 Century of Progress Exposition. At the legendary 1939 World's Fair in New York, streamlined visions of the future attracted spectators to the General Motors pavilion, where they were treated to a preview of what life would be like in the 1960s.

Hollywood embraced the style wholeheartedly because it photographed well, and the major studios built dramatic sets filled with Deco furniture, glass-block walls, porthole windows, and sweeping spiral staircases; Fred Astaire and Ginger Rogers's most famous dance routines were filmed against backdrops of pure Deco style, down to the light fixtures and patterned draperies. Movie stars were routinely shown preparing martinis in gleaming cocktail shakers or sipping coffee from cups shaped like triangles; such scenes were wonderful advertisements for the new Art Deco silver and tableware being produced by manufacturers who were routinely faced with a reluctance by many housewives to shelve some of their more traditional pieces for something more au courant.

Decorative artists working in glass, metal, and ceramics had the freedom to choose from exciting design motifs, and the culture clash of abstract and Cubist forms, machine symbols, nature motifs, and mythological images culminated in objects with designs that could be interpreted a number of ways: zigzags could be either a thunderbolt or an electronic flash; sunbursts, either a true depiction of one of nature's wonders or the flashy spoked wheel of a roadster. High-jumping gazelles could symbolize great speed or be modern adaptations of past images painted on a mummy's case like Tutankhamen's, which had been discovered in 1922;

designers delighted in playing with the possible interpretations of motifs and the opportunity for double meanings.

The quarter century roughly bridging the two world wars was a rich, exciting period for glass production. From Lalique's perfume bottles to the engraved, limited-edition glasses made by the artists Salvador Dalí, Henri Matisse, and Georgia O'Keeffe for Steuben, the pristine yet exotic designs associated with Art Deco were lavishly used on both table and decorative glass by almost all of the major glass manufac-

turers. The 1925 exposition, which provided a showplace for the latest in Art Deco wares, gave the already famous French glass designer René Lalique an opportunity to share his creative vision with a new, broader audience. Lalique's interest in glass was, first and foremost, its ability to yield to the most subtle sculptural forms and artistic nuances.

Using the *cire-perdue,* or lost-wax, process, Lalique was able to deco-

rate vases or glasses with high-relief depictions of figures or plants. At the exposition's pavilion of the Manufacture de Sèvres Lalique, a central pedestal table was covered with a full service of Lalique glass, while the ceiling, which featured molded-glass divisions, was dramatically illuminated to dazzle the crowd. Lalique's penchant for using frosted glass juxtaposed with clear glass enabled him to play with light, which was reflected in different ways from the two surfaces. Thousands of glass houses in Europe and America turned out Lalique-type glass in the 1920s and 1930s, mass-producing some of his most popular styles for the table. Today, this abundance affords us the opportunity to create tables that would be at home on an MGM movie set and gives us the materials with which to set the perfect stage for a glamorous cocktail or dinner party with friends.

**OPPOSITE:** *Ultimate Art Deco. Jean Luce's distinctive china, with its total neutral blending of bold new shapes, matte glaze, and satin-finish silver, which was designed for the 1925 Paris exposition, is displayed on a German-made worktable of high nickel content (a forerunner of stainless steel) in the kitchen of the Ford House. The glass is a Walter Dorwin Teague design that was done for Steuben in his pioneering streamline style. The flatware, originally designed by Arthur Stone in 1915–1916, was later replicated by Porter Blanchard.*

**ABOVE:** *In the 1930s, functional aluminum covers helped to keep coffee or tea warm in chunky Moderne china pots.*

**BELOW:** *A distinctive 1910 Wiener Werkstätte coffee pot with a chrome top and spout.*

A startling lesson in tableware geometry, the large
plate and coffee pot were
designed in the 1920s by
Clarice Cliff, whose cre-
ative imagination turned
an overstock of undecorated
white china bodies into a
commercial success. These
Bizarre designs are highly
collectible today. The com-
patible, yet far less costly
cups and saucers, sugar
and creamer are by Myott
from the same era.

Lalique produced an enormous range of articles in glass: vases, bowls, jewelry, lamp bases, tumblers, even clock cases. His tableware included lemonade and wine sets of decanters or jugs with glasses. Chunky models were molded with modernistic designs, while wine- glasses were often blown into molds in very-thin-walled glass, which could then be acid-etched with a decorative pattern.

The Art Deco style exerted great influence in all of the many glass houses of Europe; even the time-honored Venetian glass manufacturers of Murano, Italy, combined traditional elements with modern motifs. The Baccarat glassworks of France, the hallmark of which was pure lu- minous crystal, showed a wide range of table services, lamps, and cen- terpieces at the 1925 fair, many cut into Cubist-inspired motifs, composed of geometric circles, squares, and triangles.

Soon after the Paris exposition, America's Steuben glass produced frosted glass; acid-etched bowls with highly stylized chrysanthemums; alabaster or tinted rose-glass jars and vases featuring Moderne blos- soms; and an array of thick-walled, clear-glass or single-colored vessels with internal bubbles (including the Cintra and Cluthra lines). From the early 1930s, Steuben produced clear, often engraved and etched glass with an appeal that was chic and contemporary. It also made tableware with engraved and etched geometric designs—their Empire, Riviera, Saint Tropez, and Spiral patterns.

Douglas Nash, working for Tiffany glass, designed Chintz glass, lovely pieces with an alternating pattern of wide- and narrow-ribbed stripes of different hues. From 1932 to 1935 Nash worked for Libbey Glass, where he designed stemware in over eighty patterns in four different colors. This was truly a golden era in American glassware, as most glass companies experimented with colors, new shapes, and modern designs.

The great London department store Harrods used its fame to sponsor an exhibition of its own in 1934. The purpose was to produce a series of designs, in both glass and ceramics, that would successfully unify artists and industry, while making art wares accessible to the general public.

The English produced a spectacular amount of Art Deco china, most of which came out of the studios of two of their most innovative designers, Clarice Cliff and Susie Cooper. The jazzy beat and riotous colors of the 1920s were splashed over their teapots and teacups, sometimes fashioned in triangular shapes, so fresh in their originality they still look modern to us today; even a few pieces, such as a pair of Cliff salt and pepper shakers, would bring a touch of flapper pizzazz to a contemporary table.

Cliff began her career with simple geometric designs, incorporating sophisticated avant-garde European designs into her own spirited patterns for the

British market. Her early Bizarre line was especially popular, but, eager to branch out into more sophisticated designs, Cliff drew inspiration from the work of the French Cubists. Her series of stylized landscapes with their bright oranges, greens, and blues—House and Bridge and Orange Roof Cottage—featured pieces in unusual shapes, such as conical sugar shakers, which, while novelties at the time, have become valuable collectibles today. Clarice Cliff showed her work at the Harrods exhibition, as did two highly regarded artists from the elite band of artists and writers known as the Bloomsbury group—Vanessa Bell and Duncan Grant. The work of Bell and Grant expressed, in visual terms, the strong and steady pull away from the past, seen in the revolutionary stream-of-consciousness writings of fellow Bloomsbury member Virginia Woolf; the vivid colors and exuberant patterns captured the fast-paced literary style most dramatically and were quite popular, particularly with young couples who were always on the lookout for ways to be more modern than their parents.

Susie Cooper combined modern forms while never underrating the need for practicality; whereas some designers made triangular cup handles that were nearly impossible to grasp, Susie Cooper made certain that form never took precedence over function. Her Kestral line, with its decoration reminiscent of the abstract artist Piet Mondrian featured vegetable dishes with bowl-shaped lids that could be upturned to rest on the table while vegetables were being served—or the lid

**LEFT:** *In these photographs are Tiffany and Gorham iced-tea spoon straws and grill forks, a Whiting Martelé pick, and an unusual silver spoon shaped like a leaf.*

**OPPOSITE:** *The sun, sea, and personality of California were captured in the Catalina Ware of the 1920s, shown here on a sun-dappled table set for lunch on the patio.*

could be used separately as another dish entirely; the spouts on her coffee pots and teapots were designed to pour well; and handles had to fit comfortably and securely in the hand.

Many companies, including Moorcroft and Poole pottery, filled the demand for decorative figurines and items such as bookends in stylized animal forms, vases in Cubist-inspired shapes and modernist sculptures of fashionably dressed and coiffed young women. While many consumers stayed true to the delicate rose patterns produced by such venerable china companies as Spode, Copeland, and Royal Doulton, there was a concerted effort by even the most conservative makers to incorporate Art Deco patterns into their repertoires, particularly after 1930. Subtly banded wares with painted wavy lines, polka dots, "flirts" (a hand-painted dash like an elongated teardrop), and geometric landscapes were often painted on a ribbed body. Catalina ware, made during the 1930s, popularized flamboyant colors and is highly collectible today; it looks wonderful when various colors are mixed within each place setting.

For the most part, however, the very bright colors associated with Art Deco china were gradually replaced during the middle to late 1930s by such subtle colors as gray, brown, pink, yellow, and purplish brown—the palette of choice for the remarkably talented and unique American designer Russell Wright, whose 1939 tableware pattern for Steubenville pottery, American Modern, is coveted by collectors today who see it as one of the icons of decorative style in America. An influx of imported porcelain, notably from Austria and Japan after World War I, brought a halt to the manufacture of fancy porcelain in the United States, with many large manufacturers adapting to this change by turning out rugged and practical table china for restaurants and hotels; one exception was

**OPPOSITE AND ABOVE:**
*Art Deco whimsy is captured in Bauer's Ring Ware pottery of the 1930s. The green and clear Bakelite-handled flatware once belonged to the comedian Lou Costello. The table is set on the stunning patio of the Storer House by Frank Lloyd Wright.*

Lenox, which continued to produce high-style porcelain tablewares.

Silver is a material that was particularly well suited to the Art Deco style; it could be made to reverberate with an intense feeling of dizzying speed, and it gleamed like the spires of the Chrysler Building on a sunny day. The Wiener Werkstätte, inspired by the German Expressionists, had laid the groundwork for innovative silver design by producing hammered wares in rigid geometric forms, and the rest of Europe soon followed with handwork that was unmistakably modern. Designers could sculpt silver into fresh adaptations of ancient Egyptian, classical Greek, pre-Columbian, tribal African, French Baroque, and even Rococo styles, creating coffee sets, tableware, cigarette cases, and cocktail shakers that looked very twentieth century.

The Danish silversmith Georg Jensen displayed his work at the pivotal 1925 exposition in Paris. His style was unmistakable; his centerpieces, bowls, tureens, candelabra, and coffee and tea services were finely embellished with finials, handles, stems, and his distinctive berry and tendril decoration. Often, Jensen applied semiprecious stones, such as amber, to his pieces; his Art Deco flatware, with its floral, beaded, or geometric decorations on the handles was exquisitely made and is highly collectible today.

In America, the major silver makers had a peculiar love-hate relationship with the Art Deco style; they were at once charmed and wary of it because they feared that most Americans, while appreciating the slick surfaces and geometric shapes of Art Deco in their cars and appliances, preferred traditional styles for their silver tea and coffee service, an expensive item that was often purchased to last a lifetime. This dilemma was addressed by some of America's major manufacturers by producing smaller, purely decorative pieces or coffee and cocktail sets in the Art Deco style.

Tiffany & Co.'s ten-piece Art Deco silver cocktail set studded with cabochon emeralds was a great success at the New York World's Fair in 1939, the same year that a particularly gifted designer, Albert Barney, made a glorious sterling silver Art Deco coffee set that was adorned with touches of jade for the famous firm. Nonetheless, Tiffany, like most American silver companies, reluctantly produced pure modernist designs and went so far as to advertise its Century flatware as a pattern that was modern without the extreme angularity often associated with Art Deco style, assuring customers that "its classic simplicity will allow it to be used in harmony with period silver of the plainer styles as well as with silver of modern design."

Still, some magnificent Art Deco silver *was* made in America, most particularly Erik Magnussen's designs for Gorham. His work was strikingly different from the academic and Colonial Revival lines Gorham had been manufacturing at the time. Cubic, Magnussen's unique coffee service, featured flat, shiny silver areas contrasted with triangles of gilt and oxidized brown. While the geometric abstraction of the forms used can be traced directly to Cubism's founding fathers Georges Braque, Pablo Picasso, and Juan Gris, the spirit of the design conjures up the hectic pace of city life, and Cubic was eventually renamed The Lights and Shadows of Manhattan. Further tapping the urban landscape for inspiration, Gorham produced a set of serving pieces called Manhattan, which paid homage to the New York skyline, complete with skyscraper-decorated handles. The beauty and dynamic mood set by

**OPPOSITE:** *A tea and coffee service by Christofle echoes the shape of the portholes on the* Queen Mary.

**BELOW:** *Here is a sophisticated mélange of styles: In Deco, the Libbey silver-edged and monogrammed amethyst glassware, and International Silver's 1930 Wedgwood pattern flatware, made for the William Fisher family (one of the seven automotive Fisher brothers of Detroit); Arts and Crafts silver napkin rings; and silver Beaux-Arts candlesticks with Adam-style swags.*

this silver evoke the breakneck pace of city life; today, even a table set in a quiet hamlet or sedate suburb can capture some of the hustle and bustle of a metropolis with a few pieces of Cubic or Manhattan silver flatware, or a Tiffany Art Deco coffee pot or set of candlesticks.

International Silver of America hired the Finnish architect Eliel Saarinen to produce flatware that featured simple, elongated lines at once futuristic and elegant. Saarinen, who started the Arts and Crafts Movement in Finland, was already well known in America in the 1930s because of his work at the Cranbrook Academy in Bloomfield Hills, Michigan, where he designed many of the buildings (as well as a home for himself and his family) on the 300-acre campus. The Saarinen house, which serves as a backdrop for many of the photographs in this book, is home to some of his most beautiful silver designs for International Silver, including a coffee urn, tray, creamer, and sugar bowl that juxtapose graceful spheres with angular handles. Saarinen's work combines the best of sedate Scandinavian design with the restless energy of modern industrialized times, and remains classic, never dated—the mark of the true genius. Saarinen's wife and daughter designed all of the textiles in the house, even the place mats, while his son, Eero, became famous in his own right as an architect. As Saarinen's work evolved, so did that of Frank Lloyd Wright, who—unlike his fellow architects Greene and Greene, who fashioned each house like a fine piece of furniture—experimented with a variety of materials, including stone and poured concrete.

The joyous spirit that was at the very heart of the Art Deco style unfortunately was made to yield to the steady, unrelenting realities of yet another world war. The basic materials necessary for the production of the decorative arts were, understandably, appropriated to the manufacture of goods for the war effort. While the war sidetracked the roaring streamlined train that was Art Deco, the pulse that fueled the style still manages to beat loud and steady today, a testament to its timeless appeal.

**OPPOSITE:** *This sleek sophisticated demitasse set by Carleton from the 1920s, which is owned by the Saarinen family, captures the timeless mood of a 1930s Rudolph Knorlein sculpture.*

# LIGHT FARE

Between 1900 and World War I the state of womanhood was altered forever by a variety of factors that eased many of the restrictions that had been part of the Victorian woman's way of life as more and more women now ventured outside the home to work or to participate in causes like temperance and suffrage. During the Great War itself, women valiantly served on the battlefield as nurses or, on the home front, filled many of the jobs that had been vacated by their husbands or brothers, who had been called into combat. Their patriotism and bravery earned for them an increased respect that not only gave them in 1920 the right to vote in the United States, but also gave them a new voice and expanded freedom of expression both in the home and in the workplace, where many women increasingly found

themselves promoted from menial jobs to positions of greater responsibility. The heightened self-confidence and imaginative spirit that was so much a part of this appropriately named Progressive Era was reflected in this period's whimsical tablewares, which were well suited for the rapidly changing, increasingly modern lifestyle.

The profusion of employment opportunities available in a society becoming ever more industrialized lured many domestic workers to what they considered to be more glamorous work with higher pay. By the end of the twenties, the number of live-in servants, who had been a fixture in many middle-class homes up until that time, had greatly diminished, and they were mainly employed by families of greater financial means. Of course, the Fords, the Gambles, and the Booths continued to retain many servants and usually a French cook with whom Madame could sit down and plan a suitably impressive Continental-style luncheon menu for the members of her women's club.

A fine butler was adept at arranging a pretty breakfast tray set and would take great pains to create a pretty place setting for the lady of the house, who was sitting in bed waiting for her first meal of the day. A tap on the door, responded to by a resounding "Enter!" and the carefully composed tray, with a copy of the day's newspaper rolled up and tucked in at the side, was ceremoniously placed before her. Such a morning offering might include a delicate Shelley or Wedgwood breakfast set; a Tiffany Favrile glass filled with freshly squeezed orange juice; well-polished Reed and Barton sterling silver flatware with which to cut and butter a croissant; a Lalique vase with a few flowers that matched the hand-painted flowers on the china; and a finely embroidered linen place

**PRECEDING PAGES:** *The breakfast porch at the Gamble House is set with a cheerful mix of Adams Titianware china from the 1930s and red and yellow Bakelite flatware. The original Gustav Stickley oak table and L.J.G. Stickley chairs were chosen by the Greenes, the architects of the house.*

**OPPOSITE:** *In the original Craftsman kitchen of the Gamble House a table holds a "bachelor" set by Bisto from 1929 and Jadite kitchenware.*

**ABOVE:** *Cheese is stored in an 1890s covered dish in the original 1914 ice box at the Lanterman House.*

**ABOVE:** *Three breakfast trays are daintily set at the Ford House with vintage Porthault linens and Shelley china.*

**OPPOSITE:** *In the butler's pantry at the Ford House, a green lacquer tray holds Tiffany parfait and coupe glasses, a dessert plate for a morning croissant, Porter Blanchard flatware, and a small epergne filled with Mrs. Ford's favorite flower, yellow tea roses.*

mat and napkin. While sipping her tea or coffee, the mistress of the house planned her day, which might include a dress fitting, an early-afternoon appointment with a curator of a museum to arrange the specifics of an exhibition for which she was lending some of her prized paintings, a late-afternoon bridge game with her best lady friends, and a fancy dinner in the evening at which she and her husband would be entertaining a visiting diplomat from overseas.

For the more typical women, who inhabited the sometimes financially rough waters of the middle class, and for single young girls on their own (called bachelor girls by the press), the joys and benefits of earning one's own living were powerful magnets that pulled many a country girl into the heart of the big city. The rush off to work made the languid Victorian breakfasts, with their course after course of heavy food and multiple plates, glasses, cups, forks, and spoons, very much a thing of the past.

*Modern Antiques for the Table*

*Light Fare*

For those who punched a time clock, breakfasts were now a bowl of cereal, a bit of toast, coffee, and perhaps a soft-boiled egg quickly swallowed in time to make the 7 A.M. express. China companies, like Bisto, Adams, and Royal Winton, among many others, responded to the change in lifestyle by manufacturing what came to be called breakfast or bachelor sets; designed for one, they contained a matching sugar bowl, creamer, cup and saucer, cereal bowl, and a 9-inch plate.

While the frantic pace of a working life was a strong motive for cutting back on the size of one's breakfast during the early years of the new century, there was another, perhaps greater, reason: the newer, more body-revealing fashions worn by women, who were now becoming more involved in sports like tennis and golf, had replaced the corset that had once cinched even less-than-perfect bodies into an hourglass shape. This meant that one's natural figure was more noticeable and one had to watch her weight to maintain a well-proportioned shape. Health-food advocates, like Dr. John Harvey Kellogg of Battle Creek Sanitorium, who developed cornflakes, inspired a minor revolution in how women ate and in how they chose to feed their families, and lighter meals became the order of the day.

While married working women might have been more rushed than their mothers had been, many of them found it hard to ignore the importance of setting a pretty table for their husbands in the breakfast nook by the window, and so they might use Mother's favorite Wedgwood with the pretty rose pattern, or perhaps her Haviland Enchantment wedding china, or the few Gien Art Nouveau plates left by a grandmother; faceted Venetian glass goblets, dutifully polished silver flatware, and a floral arrangement would set just the right mood before a woman went to catch the train into the city. For the most part, however, the casualness of the fashions that had replaced the stiff garments of the Victorian and Edwardian eras was matched by a new, free spirit in setting the table as well; gaily checked or cheerfully patterned tablecloths, and colorful plates, pitchers, and coffee pots often took the place of finer china, which, more and more, was reserved for company or special occasions. Bakelite- (the first synthetic plastic, developed in 1907) or ivorine-handled flatware was used more and more often, while the silver flatware was left undisturbed in its velvet-lined wooden box, and Depression Glass was used every day, while the expensive Steuben crystal was kept in the dining-room breakfront. The new informality (and lack of servants) even made it suddenly all right to recruit one's guests to help transport their dishes to the kitchen at the meal's end, and to help their hostess wash and dry while chatting over a sink of soapy water.

Many women were employed, during the twenties and thirties, in the studios of china designers like England's Clarice Cliff, Charlotte Rhead, and Susie Cooper, and, in America, by Dorothy Thorpe, who was one of the first women designers to have their very own boutiques in fashionable department stores like Bullock's in California. Although each of these designers had a distinct personality, there was a common denominator that unified their styles—an inventiveness expressed in whimsical shapes and joyful colors. The manufacturers of Chintz ware, which was mass-produced and very popular, never could have managed to keep up with their orders if it had not been for the scores of young girls who painstakingly applied the transfers that created the profusely flowering patterns that were the rage during

**ABOVE AND RIGHT:**
*Wedgwood's enameled Old Rose pattern and pale faceted Venetian glass set for lunch at Cranbrook House on a quilted mat, with mother-of-pearl-handled flatware.*

Having lunch with
Dorothy Thorpe circa
1930 on her hand-
painted jade butterfly
china, etched glasses,
and martini pitcher.
Terrapin forks, silver
shells, and an Ernest
Batchelder trumpet
vase complete a
delightful setting.

**ABOVE:** *Clarice Cliff's whimsical Bizarre 1930s cup and saucer, conical salt shakers, and honey pot of the 1930s mix playfully with a Czech cruet set and an American cookie jar from the same era.*

**OPPOSITE:** *Evoking images of country life in Provence, French Coq Vin china and red and white Bakelite flatware were chosen for an omelet brunch. A toy collection, displayed with pride, provides an amusing background.*

the twenties and thirties, and which are currently enjoying a renaissance with today's collectors.

The shift of women from doing full-time housekeeping to working outside the home created a need for new ways to help lighten their workload at home, and magazines and newspapers advertised all types of gadgets and gizmos designed to save time. One twenties cookbook, deploring the woeful scarcity of servants, dubbed the housewife "Mrs. Three-In-One," who, like today's superwoman, had to juggle work and home responsibilities. Perhaps the greatest electric "servant" of all was the refrigerator, which made it possible to keep foods fresh for much longer periods of time than had the big old icebox, and enabled women to prepare some meals ahead. Food editors of popular women's magazines, such as *Good Housekeeping*, responded to readers' requests for easy menus for entertaining in "maid-less" households; the answer for many was Jell-O. The convenience of boxed, easy-to-prepare gelatin created a glut of Jell-O–based salads during the twenties and thirties, which found favor at the kitchen table for an afternoon snack for children returning from school, as well as for ladies' luncheons. Companies like Heisey responded to the ubiquitous radio advertisements for Jell-O by stepping up production of sherbet glasses, sometimes designed to fit into sherbet plates, that were just the right depth for serving a big dollop of the jiggly-wiggly stuff, crowned, of course, by a heady topping of freshly whipped cream and a maraschino cherry.

In the 1920s, the exuberance that was so much a part of the jazz age expressed itself in bright colors and whimsical objects, like roosters and chickens (perfect for serving the rage of the twenties, chicken à la king), as well as in playful shapes. Nowhere was this more evident than in Clarice Cliff's Bizarre china, which was mass-produced in England and

widely sold in the United States. One can easily picture young children playing games with salt and pepper shakers shaped like pointed party hats or stealing a few gingersnaps from a cookie jar featuring a cow jumping over the moon while their mother's back was turned because she was making a batch of waffles on her new, handy-dandy electric waffle machine. Cliff's vibrant oranges and springtime greens set off by touches of jet black went particularly well with the red and green Bakelite-handled flatware that is so collectible today. In the 1920s, her reflective lusters, bright colors, and hand-painted patterns, often of simple landscapes or country cottages, were immensely popular, while in the thirties, Shelley's, Royal Doulton's, and Susie Cooper's more delicate palettes, often sprinkled with frisky polka dots, became increasingly popular.

Whimsical landscapes on china were favorites during the 1920s and 1930s with companies like Royal Albert, Paragon, and Aynsley, which made Deco-inspired square plates overgrown with foxgloves, water lilies, and assorted blossoms that conjured up lazy walks through New York's Central Park or London's Kew Gardens. The shadings of pink and green used on china sets went beautifully with the pink and green Depression Glass that graced many dining tables during this period, and a new color, orange, appeared on these cheerful sets as well.

For those who could not afford to visit resorts like The Greenbrier, good times might be had by inviting friends to stop by, on those cherished days off, for a light lunch. The dainty food served in the ubiquitous tearooms of the 1920s, or in department-store dining rooms, or in popular coffee shops like Rumpelmayer's and Schrafft's—salmon croquettes, date-nut bread and cream cheese sandwiches, creamed sweetbreads in patty shells, and an endless variety of icebox cakes, accompanied by pots of hot tea and coffee or pitchers of icy lemonade and iced tea—provided a wealth of ideas for women looking for just the right thing to serve the next time "the girls" came over for bridge, mahjongg, or just some good old-fashioned gossip.

**OPPOSITE, ABOVE LEFT:** *Art Nouveau's love of all things natural is expressed by George Jones hand-painted, leafy fern ice cream dishes and a Minton teapot with a bamboo handle and spout set out on a bamboo mat.* **ABOVE RIGHT:** *A collection of lighthearted landscape china includes Blossom Time and Foxglove by Royal Albert, a water lily design by Paragon, Tea Post by Tunstall, and a pretty green plate with floral handles by Showyer & Son.* **BELOW LEFT:** *A greenhouse is the setting for a cup of tea shaped like a flower that was a gift from Henry Ford to the owner of Van Dyke Place.* **BELOW RIGHT:** *Copeland Art Nouveau luncheon plates, a Dresden covered square bottle used as a vase, and etched and gilded blown cranberry wineglasses capture the floral essence of Virginia Robinson's fabled flower gardens.*

A Betty Crocker booklet called the 1920s the beginning of the real cake era. Part of the reason for cake's newfound popularity was that since relatively few had servants during the twenties it became popular to have only one dish for the dessert course; because of this, the period saw a tremendous increase in cake plates and cake stands, as well as in attractive, sometimes ruffle-edged, tiered tidbit stands meant for cookies or petits fours. Cake plates ranged from 10 to 13 inches and sometimes had a groove near the rim to accommodate a metal or glass lid. They were popular giveaways, particularly during the Depression-ravaged thirties; Jeannette Glass slipped the three-footed Sunflower-pattern cake plate into 25-pound bags of flour, and nearly all their competitors did similar promotions, inserting cereal bowls into boxes of oatmeal, and giving away tumblers, pitchers, and plates with the purchase of everything from a movie ticket to a tank of gas.

Beautiful, ornately pierced silver cake servers and lavishly engraved, bright-cut cake knives were de rigueur for hostesses who enjoyed baking on their Saturdays off, and a well-dressed luncheon table always featured at least a few beautiful silver or silver-plated serving pieces. In London, at the Portobello Road Market, or at the many antiques fairs that run throughout the year in the United States, bakelite-handled, heavily engraved cake knives and servers are still readily available at good prices. On a recent trip to the Portobello Road Market, as I snatched up just such a cake knife, the proprietor informed me that I had to promise to make a sultana cake to go with the knife, just like the one his mother always made for her friends on Tuesday afternoons when they stopped over for tea and talk.

Today, a homemade strawberry shortcake served on a daintily painted cake stand, with cups of coffee, tumblers of milk, and perhaps a

*OPPOSITE AND ABOVE:*
*The sun shines through the windows of the breakfast room designed by Dorothy Draper at The Greenbrier, and filters through the cranberry Polka Dot water goblets by Pairpoint, making playful shadows on a charming table setting that mixes George Jones and Minton plates, Royal Winton Chintz ware cups and saucers, and an Art Nouveau silver coffee pot.*

**OPPOSITE:** *A wonderful collection of Chintz includes 1926 Crown Ducal Blue Chintz vases and pitchers, and Royal Winton 1934 Hazel with a black background, and a candy jar in Julia, a late but popular pattern. Much of today's prized Chintz was once just considered to be "cheap and cheerful" everyday ware. It's still cheerful but no longer cheap, especially in complete sets with original parts, or in uncommon patterns and shapes.*

*For a delightful tea, Crown Ducal's Florida pattern serves up a wordless song of the tropics, and displays a small selection of one collector's prized Chintz ware. The odd teapot is an unknown pattern by Baker and Company.*

pink glass sandwich plate piled high with watercress and cucumber sandwiches would certainly evoke the amiable, sublimely feminine world of Grandmother's favorite tearoom, where the aroma of freshly baked charlotte russes blended with the sweet scent of rosewater worn by happily chatting customers—a world that the novelist H. H. Munro, better known as Saki, adored for its "thousands of women sitting behind dainty porcelain and silver fittings, with their voices tinkling pleasantly in a cascade of questions."

Ladies' luncheons could be small, intimate affairs attended by close friends or larger, more elaborately planned events to raise money for the wide assortment of ladies' charitable organizations that proliferated during the twenties and thirties; indeed, the woman who didn't belong to a study club, sewing club, gardening or bridge club during this time was considered to be something of an oddball, for clubs offered the chance to socialize and to keep current with all the latest news, while providing the ideal place to show off that just-purchased flowery afternoon frock or darling little hat. For many the perfect china for their carefully prepared luncheons was Chintz ware—made, most notably, by the English china companies Royal Winton, Crown Ducal, James Kent, and Grimwades.

Chintz fabric goes back to the richly detailed material imported into England from India during the late seventeenth century. Europeans quickly became enamored of chintz, using it to decorate their homes, and it was inevitable that china manufacturers would find ways to duplicate the exotic yet homey floral patterns of the fabric onto hand-painted tableware. The development and perfection of transfer printing, the process by which sheets of vividly colored flower patterns were applied to the china surface, enabled china

manufacturers quickly to produce Chintz ware that was, for the most part, originally intended for seaside cottages or bungalows.

The charm of Chintz ware plates, teapots, breakfast sets, biscuit barrels, egg cups, toast racks, cheese and butter dishes, luncheon sets, and full dinner services attracted the eyes of even haughty society matrons and avant-garde sophisticates; a steady stream of requests for more and more of the beguiling china kept the big department stores well stocked with Chintz ware well into the 1940s. Not only did factories turn out new patterns at a dizzying rate, they competed with one another by creating new and interesting shapes on a regular basis. In 1922, Crown Ducal was lauded in the American press for what would come to be known as tennis or hostess sets, which included a matching cup, saucer, and tray. In 1933, it was Grimwades that was noted in an American trade journal for plates with plain embossed borders and Chintz centers; in the same year, it was also praised for its latest design, the breakfast or bedside set—a small tray with a

**ABOVE:** *Chintz ware stackable teapots like this one, which is shown both assembled and disassembled, by Royal Winton in the Stratford pattern are highly prized.*

toast rack, sugar bowl, creamer, and a little teapot, all fitted into grooves.

Royal Winton's Julia, Summertime, and Old Cottage were some of the most popular Chintz patterns of all time, but Royal Winton's Somerset, which came with either a blue or a gold trim, and Crown Ducal's Blue Chintz and Florida patterns also graced a great many tables in the 1930s, where their depictions of springtime's gay flowers helped to lift heavy hearts during the Depression. Women in England and in America were especially infatuated with Chintz ware stacking teapots, which allowed them neatly to place a teapot, creamer, and sugar bowl one on top of another. Given the immense popularity of Chintz ware, there can be no doubt that many breakfast and luncheon tables were set with the china during the 1920s and 1930s, probably with shades of glass that picked up one or two colors from the all-over patterns. Today, although prices for vintage Chintz ware have been rising steadily, there are still many bargains to be found. If one is willing to mix patterns—a cup and saucer found here, a lone cereal bowl picked up there—before long there will be enough pieces to set a charming, nostalgic table that re-calls simpler days.

The post–World War I years witnessed the first major flowering of the suburbs, pictured as elegant, exclusive communities for the wealthy or as friendly bungalow neighborhoods where middle-class families could raise their children away from the noise and sooty windowsills that came with life in the city. In the April 1906 issue of the Arts and Crafts furniture designer Gustav Stickley's magazine, *The Craftsman*, a bungalow with an open-air dining area was featured with an accompanying article expounding on the virtues of bringing the outdoors within and allowing the indoors to stretch outside. The new devotion to health and fitness that was making women lighten their meals, practice calisthenics, and

**OPPOSITE:** *A light lunch is served on the porch of Lanterman House, mixing Gien Oiseaux Art Nouveau china with green pressed-glass wines, etched and handled lemonades, and iced-tea glasses used for water. Unmatched silver-plate and ivorine utensils are simply set on a 1914 Wakefield rattan table with matching chairs.*

**ABOVE:** *For a leisurely late-afternoon rest, an Austrian demitasse service made in 1920 and set on a floral chintz cloth beneath a luxurious spread of wisteria would make anyone feel content.*

**ABOVE:** *The serene beauty of a lily pond instills this glass-topped patio table set with German plates shaped like lily pads made in 1930 by Zell. The square plates and divided serving platters were made by Winfield circa 1930–1940 for Joan Crawford. The Art Nouveau silver is by Gorham and Whiting and the salad servers by Kalo.*

**OPPOSITE:** *An 1880 bronze fountain sculpted by Edwin Lewin Funcke creates a meditative mood in this garden. The mauve plates and glasses are by Dorothy Thorpe, the pâté de verre molded dish by Daum, and the tall Venetian gold-and-amethyst glass was made in Murano in 1920. The flatware has handles made of shagreen (sharkskin).*

enter Ping-Pong tournaments expressed itself in another important way at the turn of the century and beyond—fresh air was extolled for its health-sustaining abilities, and every opportunity to get outdoors was taken. Roofed sleeping porches, which were already becoming a common feature in homes being built in 1900, were highly praised and coveted by many, including the Gamble family, as the century advanced; the two young Gamble sons slept outdoors throughout the year on the sleeping porch built onto their house in Pasadena, California, by the Greene brothers, as did many other children and adults seeking to fill their lungs with clean oxygen.

As more people left the cities and ventured into suburbia, the interest in gardening and landscape design blossomed. Whether it was a massive estate like the one built in 1911 for the department-store heir Harry Winchester Robinson and his wife, Virginia, or a humble quarter of an acre in Brooklyn, land was tilled, flowers were planted, and the pleasures of dining outdoors were wholeheartedly enjoyed. Parks, spas, and summer resorts like The Greenbrier featured elaborately landscaped grounds that provided inspiration for those intent on creating beautiful gardens of their own. World travel, engravings in garden books, and the international expositions and fairs exposed the public to exotic plants and garden ornaments from distant lands, while mail-order seed catalogs and landscaping guides offered advice for novices, giving tips on choosing flowers suitable for their site and on the appropriate tools considered essential for the well-tended garden. Porches, piazzas, pergolas, terraces, and trellises soared in popularity, as did woven furniture; rattan easy chairs, dining-room sets, lampshades, swings, and tea carts were inexpensive but sturdy, and were used both indoors and out by the family and to entertain guests.

A table set for two out on the porch on a lazy Sunday morning, with pretty Chintz ware teacups and cranberry glasses to catch the sun and a big silver pot filled with hot coffee, could make any hardworking couple forget the office, especially in a setting with a neatly mowed lawn and manicured flower beds. In addition to enjoying outdoor meals with their families, women delighted in entertaining their lady friends in the shade of a tree, where they could show off their very latest rosebush and a carefully prepared table setting. To complement the garden setting, many

hostesses chose tableware that featured flora and fauna—such as Royal Worcester's Marseilles china in sunny yellow with a trellis cartouche border and delicately painted rose-filled baskets, George Jones's exquisite hand-painted fern ice-cream dishes, Dorothy Thorpe's unusual mauve-colored floral design plates, and a Minton teapot with a molded ceramic bamboo handle and spout. Cambridge, Fostoria, and Tiffin made glassware etched with apple blossoms and other springtime posies on colored glass that echoed the hues of garden flowers. Often, clever hostesses used celery vases or cake stands to hold fresh flowers or fruits such as lemons and limes on their rattan or wrought-iron tables out on the flagstone patio; the gift of being able to see an alternate use for a piece of china, glass, and silver has always been a useful one that often leads to the creation of the prettiest, most eye-pleasingly creative tables.

A pattern like Flower Pagodas by Royal Doulton, paired with

Steuben jade-colored lemonade glasses, bamboo-handled flatware, and Oriental boy and girl salt and pepper shakers would have made a splendid choice for a mah-jongg party or for a dinner under the stars, brightly lit by Chinese paper lanterns—during the twenties or now. Hostesses engaged in friendly competition with one another, trying to come up with unusual table settings for their club breakfasts or luncheons, and flower arranging was studied by women wanting to display the glorious flowers they had grown; an outdoor table would not have been complete without a pretty glass vase or a silver one holding an attractive floral spray.

For those lucky (and wealthy) enough to have a swimming pool or a pond on their grounds, the entertaining possibilities escalated, and pool parties were the height of chic during the 1930s. The often-photographed pool at San Simeon in California, Randolph Hearst's castle built for his paramour Marion Davies, as well as the glorious Italianate pool pavilion belonging to Virginia and Harry Robinson, and James Oviatt's pool on his penthouse roof terrace were the sites of soirees that attracted many of Hollywood's biggest stars; the glamour of those parties enticed many to set a table next to their own modest swimming pool. Etched iced-tea glasses and plates in pale blue by Fostoria were the pièce de résistance at such get-togethers, their fragile color capturing the hue of the pool's water and the clear sky above.

The graceful blend of landscape design and architecture at the Robinson estate in Los Angeles, which is listed in the National Register of Historic Places and can today be visited by the public, reflects an era of gracious living and legendary hospitality. The regal Mediterranean Clas-

sic Revival house was built in 1911 by the bride's father, the architect Nathaniel Dryden, as a wedding present for the newly married couple. The expansive lawns, majestic palms, and more than six sloping acres boasting a variety of more than one thousand species of plants were designed by Charles Gibbs Adams, a well-known landscape architect of the 1920s and 1930s. Quiet spots for sitting, reflecting, and spreading a cloth out for an impromptu picnic abound, and such a lush setting demands the finest dining accoutrements—no paper plates here! A late-morning brunch might have featured a silver strawberry server, with two fluted bowls overflowing with gargantuan homegrown strawberries, as well as large serving spoons, little bowls filled with sugar, filigree napkin rings wrapped around crochet-edged napkins, monogrammed gold-embossed champagne glasses, a silver champagne bucket, and a silver bud vase holding one of Mrs. Robinson's prize camellias.

The heat of the midday sun has been the impetus for many novel settings for outdoor dining, and one of the most beloved plants of the 1920s and 1930s, the wisteria, provided an abundance of shade beneath its outstretched blooms; demitasse for two under the cool umbrella of a wisteria vine is an experience we all can still enjoy today. A variety of mauve- and lilac-tinted china, both old and new, along with similarly colored Depression Glass and perhaps a few cherished pieces of Gorham Martelé silver embossed with grape clusters, or an Art Nouveau set of silver berry spoons would successfully capture the romance and grandeur of dining alfresco during the era that saw Gertrude Ederle swim the English Channel, Amelia Earhart take to the skies, and Shirley Temple tap her way into the hearts of millions.

# The Movable Feast

As the twentieth century dawned, that "newfagled contraption," the automobile, as well as those enduring bastions of sophisticated travel, the railroads and the dazzling transatlantic ocean liners, necessitated the creation of modern ways for people to dine while in motion, and a new era of movable feasting was born. When at all possible, people tried to eat en route in much the same way they dined at home; while this could be achieved by dining off fine china and sipping sherry from crystal stemware aboard one of the turn-of-the-century's grander railroad dining cars or on a streamlined ship outfitted with a sumptuous starboard restaurant that was just past the swimming pool and shuffleboard courts, it was a bit of a challenge when people were wedged into the very limited confines of a Model T.

In America, Henry Ford's Tin Lizzie rolled off the assembly line in 1913, creating a new way for people from all walks of life to see the great sights of the United States, such as the Grand Canyon, Niagara Falls, and, in 1923, the towering letters spelling out HOLLYWOOD in the hills overlooking the mansions of Beverly Hills' biggest movie stars. For those whose homes were too far away from the streetcar's tracks, the automobile was a valuable lifeline connecting them to theaters, museums, and department stores.

The turn of the century saw a transformation in the world of leisure activity as paid vacations and summer breaks became the norm for an increasingly large segment of the population. A variety of vacation choices was available: one could visit a health spa or one of the mountain resorts devoted to the revitalization of often harried city dwellers, spend time at the newly created entertainment mecca, Atlantic City, ride the roller coaster at Coney Island, or, perhaps, visit one of Henry Morrison Flagler's hotels on Florida's east coast. The wealthy usually chose to sail to Europe to see the sights and collect unusual souvenirs to share with friends when they returned home.

Ford's beloved invention inspired the young and old, the rich and the middle class, to don goggles and driving gloves and, with map in hand, set out to discover America. Taking along a box of fried chicken, a jumble of forks and spoons, and a Thermos of hot coffee, a family of modest means could meander down country roads bordered with brilliant autumn leaves and stop by the side of the road for an informal picnic; auto-camping became a fad in the early 1900s, with scores of nature-loving families pitching tents and sleeping under the stars. The wealthier motorist would undoubtedly pack his roadster with an Abercrombie & Fitch woven-wicker hamper; serving as a portable larder, it would be fully outfitted so that he and his family could dine alfresco with the same high-quality tablewares they used in their formal dining room at home.

PRECEDING PAGES: *The Ford family picnic hamper by Abercrombie & Fitch is ready to be stowed in their classic 1941 gray Lincoln Continental, all set to take to the open road in search of brilliant fall foliage.*

OPPOSITE: *Grafton and Sons 1920s china tea set goes "modern" with square-shaped plates decorated with cheerful landscapes.*

A horse-drawn carriage used to transport guests for leisurely rides and picnics at The Greenbrier. A mix of Minton Birds and Cockatrice plates and Cambridge etched Apple Blossom yellow glass provide a colorful setting for an alfresco lunch.

By 1920, two million Model Ts were being sold annually in the United States, making the nation truly a car culture. As the decade progressed, more and more luxury cars—by Dodge, Chrysler, Packard, Hudson, Nash, Studebaker, and the former race-driving brothers, the Duesenbergs—were being made to keep up with a society overwhelmed by an insatiable wanderlust.

Many china companies responded to the rage for traveling by designing attractive breakfast, bachelor, tête-à-tête, or tea-for-two sets that were easily packed. Stacking Chintz ware teapots by Royal Winton, so collectible today, cleverly combined form and function, making them perfect for a day out on the dusty road when a nice cup of tea certainly would have hit the spot about four o'clock. The geometry of some of the china made during the 1920s and 1930s made it

**ABOVE:** *A flock of birds is captured in this etched glassware. Bird of Paradise iced-tea glasses by Lotus and Persian Pheasant water goblets and pitcher by Tiffin add to the glamour of taking the waters at The Greenbrier.*

possible to wedge pieces together to conserve space that was needed in the trunk or in the back on the rumble seat for suitcases and Junior's Flexible Flyer or tricycle.

During the 1920s, International Silver produced a series of machine-made, hand-finished, four-part tea services, sometimes with Bakelite or ivorine handles, that were made to sit snugly in a fitted tray, just right for a bumpy car or train ride. The French silver company Christofle made similar tea and coffee services in stark geometric forms, sometimes incorporating new materials like plate glass or exotic Makassar ebony for the handles, which were often set perpendicular to the body of the pot. Collapsible silver traveling cups, like those taken by the British to their outposts in India and Africa, also became popular at this time.

The golden age of the railroads, which had begun in the late nineteenth century, still had plenty of "steam" left in it as the new century dawned, but to compete with the ever-mounting numbers of cars taking to the road, the big railroad companies had to pull out all the stops to keep their clientele faithful. They did this by creating trains that were very much like grand hotels on wheels, complete with deep pile carpeting, lavishly appointed dining cars with fine china, silver, and crystal on the tables, barbershops, cocktail lounges, chandeliers, and well-stocked wine bins, as well as countless other luxuries aimed at drivers unhappily contending with muddy roads, balloon tires that often went flat, and a lack of decent lodging or restaurants along sometimes primitive thoroughfares.

Wealthy passengers—like Barbara Hutton, William K. Vanderbilt, the Astors, or the automobile barons Edsel Ford and Horace Dodge—could reserve (or buy) one or even a string of private railroad cars. Their every whim would have been catered

White Sulphur Springs Depot circa 1931

to by a solicitous staff dressed in crisp, freshly starched uniforms; such journeys made "getting there" as glamorous as "being there," but the train ride from Point A to Point B, even for those of much more modest means, was certain to be a memorable adventure. The mystery writer Agatha Christie, who set some of her famous novels, like *Murder on the Orient Express,* aboard trains, argued that railroads possess a charm and appeal not to be found in any other mode of transportation; if one pictures Cary Grant and Eva Marie Saint coyly chatting over cups of coffee on a moving train in Alfred Hitchcock's *North by Northwest,* or Carole Lombard and John Barrymore's screwball antics aboard one of the most famous trains of all time, *The Twentieth Century Limited,* one is hard put to disagree.

On Barbara Hutton's private railroad car
gold-washed silver spoons, initialed flatware, and gold-banded Tiffin glasses are
combined with Venetian champagnes and
finger bowls, and assorted monogrammed
china, to recall the golden age of rail-
roading.

**ABOVE:** *Sheffield silver-plate warming covers made for the Cunard line fit perfectly on contemporary Deco-style dinner plates.*

**OPPOSITE:** *Here we are at poolside on the* Queen Mary *in front of the towel booth. Original bi-color slatted chairs are next to a pull-up table set with Deco china banded in fire-engine red, Elkington Hotel silver water and ice buckets, a Gorham Deco silver bowl, and tall color-banded water tumblers.*

To supplement their profits, many railroad owners bought properties that were easily reached by their trains; such localities were then advertised with elaborately produced full-color brochures given out at the railroad station (or at gas stations, where weary drivers were at their most vulnerable). The Chesapeake and Ohio Railroad owned The Greenbrier in West Virginia, one of America's most luxurious resorts, which catered to a clientele that came to enjoy the mountain climate, sample the mineral waters, and mingle with fashionably dressed financiers, Southern belles, and the occasional movie star. The same Greenbrier that had once seen its guests pull up in horse-drawn carriages eagerly awaited a new crop of customers arriving by train or automobile. Once on terra firma, patrons were pampered with fine meals served on impeccably dressed tables in the main dining room, while the younger, more limber set might choose to sink down onto a pretty cloth set out on the great lawn, where they could simultaneously savor the food and the splendors of the surrounding landscape.

For those who favored the open sea to the clatter of train wheels or the bumpety-bump of automobiles, there was yet another way to see the world—aboard an ocean liner like the *Titanic,* which tragically sank in 1912 on her maiden voyage. Her passengers were described by a journalist of the time as "a large set of fashionable people living an international life of their own—restlessly migrating from country to country, from season to season. They were extravagant, frivolous, but perhaps the most cosmopolitan group the world has ever seen." The *Titanic* was lavishly appointed with dinner china by Royal Crown Derby that featured gold-rimmed edges with green garlands on a white ground; between the fifth and seventh courses of an eleven-course dinner, a palate cleanser called punch romaine was served in matching dessert cups. After dinner, passengers could have visited the ship's reception room, where they could drink coffee while listening

to the ship's orchestra (which is rumored to have steadfastly continued to play as the great ship sank) or get up and dance to lyrical
Strauss waltzes.

In 1936, people hoping to experience the ultimate in luxury
ocean travel would certainly have booked passage on England's pride
of the ocean, the *Queen Mary,* for she was larger, faster, and perhaps
even grander than the *Titanic.* With her exquisite Art Deco interior,
designed by the finest artists and craftsmen of the day, Cunard's *Queen
Mary* became a symbol of good taste in the world of first-class travel,
and she saw many moguls, celebrities, and modest folk proudly strut
up her gangplank and set sail upon the choppy waters of the Atlantic.

The Royal Marine Band played on the sun deck of the great ship as
she traversed the sea from Southampton to New York, calling her passengers to dinner either in the grand dining room or in the chic Verandah Grill, where a cocktail lounge and dance floor kept things hopping
well into the wee hours of the morning. For those wishing to end the
day on a quieter note, a late-night tête-à-tête over a cup of coffee and a
light tidbit could be enjoyed at a table set on the promenade deck,
against a spectacular wooden mural made up of all the many different
types of wood that were used in decorating the ship. A cheerful Bavarian tea set with radiating ribs that mirrored the radiating sun pictured
in the mural would be a perfect choice for such a cozy table, and a hefty
ashtray would have been thoughtfully provided if the diners were cigar-
smoking card players looking to gamble away the night.

Many silver companies, particularly during the lean Depression
years, supplemented their incomes by designing flatware and hollowware for trains, ocean liners, and hotels. In 1923, R. Wallace and
Sons refitted the dining rooms of the ocean liner S.S. *Leviathan* with
more than sixty thousand pieces of silverware, while in 1938, the International Silver Company (whose Hotel Division generated a large
proportion of its income) made a pattern named for *The Twentieth Cen-*

**OPPOSITE AND ABOVE:**
*This setting of the* Queen
Mary's *Kosher china, dairy or
meat, is in the Verandah Room.
Stuart crystal in the Waves
pattern and Elkington flatware, serving domes, and
tureens sit upon a linen cloth
with a wave design. The white
chairs are original to the ship,
as are the 1938 menu card and
table marker.*

*tury Limited,* one of the most streamlined and sophisticated trains ever to hit the tracks. Silverware used on trains and ships was usually monogrammed with the initials of the establishment for which it was made, and it is sought after by collectors or by people simply wanting to capture some of the glamour of the golden age of train and ship travel.

On the *Queen Mary,* breakfast was served on china that was up-to-the-minute chic, like Foley's clever little tea sets that were made to be stored pieced together somewhat like a jigsaw puzzle, just right for packing into tight spots like a ship's galley or a cramped, wooden-handled tin picnic basket. A platter of fresh fruit (ripened to perfection in the ship's fruit-ripening room) was accompanied by silver tongs and slotted berry spoons, as well as fruit knives with ornamental mother-of-pearl, bone, or ivory handles and specially designed narrow, pointed silver blades for paring the skin off fruit. Today, the silver that was once elaborately designed for the serving of fruit can be used on the breakfast table or for serving cheese at cocktail parties, where guests will certainly be delighted by the attention to detail silver makers paid in order to dress a table according to established rules of etiquette.

The *Queen Mary*'s huge promenade deck was, with its many fashionable shops, travel bureau, and restaurants, somewhat of a maritime version of London's Regent Street or Rome's Via Veneto, and yet, for those not interested in shopping, hundreds of comfortable folding deck chairs, lined up side by side, often encouraged shipboard friendships or romances that would last a lifetime; many were the times that a couple might meet while lazily stretched out, reading the latest

Dashiell Hammett novel and contentedly sipping some hot broth. As hard as the battle for winning a lady's heart might be aboard ship, the battle fought by manufacturers for producing the tableware used on the *Queen Mary* could be even fiercer. Competitions for such an honor (and for such wonderful advertising of one's product) were keen indeed, and many major companies of the day championed their wares hoping to win favor with the North Atlantic's *Queen*. Jackson and Gosling Limited of Stoke on Trent made much of the china for the ship, while most of the twenty-two thousand pieces of table glass and crystal aboard was manufactured by Stuart and Sons of Stourbridge. Interestingly, the ship kept a separate kosher set of dishes to oblige those adhering to these dietary laws; Ridgway plates with a black-and-white Deco border, as well as separate sets of Elkington flatware, kosher pots, and separate dome-lidded serving dishes were used.

When summertime temperatures soared and delicate complexions called for a respite from the sun, the *Queen Mary*'s pool was the place to be and to be seen. The pool was set within a room adorned with etched-glass panels of fish that captured the look of a massive seawater aquarium; surrounding the pool were many little niches where a cocktail or a bottle of mineral water and a few choice canapés could be taken. Wide-silver-banded china ringed with zingy bands of red complemented the slatted pool chairs of aqua and fire-engine red, and the pull-up tables, while an Elkington silver ice bucket would keep beverages cold until bathers were all toweled off and ready to drink from one of Stuart and Sons' beautiful crystal glasses, etched with a fitting pattern of waves.

To capture the breezy style of the *Queen Mary* and of the stately private yachts owned by the

Fords, the Rockefellers, Anna Thompson Dodge, and her good friend Marjorie Merriweather Post, one need assemble only a few pieces of china and elegant stemware perhaps salvaged from one of the great hotels of the era, and glasses the color of the ocean at dawn by Fostoria, Cambridge, Tiffin, or any of the many makers of Depression-era elegant stemware, to create a table that would be seaworthy. In the 1920s, at her Detroit estate, Rose Terrace (which was unfortunately torn down in the 1970s), Anna Thompson Dodge's sumptuous dinners and table settings were as talked about as those aboard the family's private yacht, the *Delphine,* the second-largest private yacht in the world at the time (only the English royal yacht *Britannia* was larger). For on-board luncheons before a friendly game of bridge, Mrs. Dodge might have used place settings of the *Delphine's* exclusively designed bone china by Cauldon; edged with thick sterling silver and decorated with a silver flag and a hand-painted depiction of the ship's banner, it would have been accompanied by Gorham silver flatware (bearing a delicately engraved *D* for Dodge). To conjure up a seaside ambience, Mrs. Dodge liked to use the miniature sterling-silver and twenty-four-karat-gold replica of the *Delphine's* dinghy as a jaunty centerpiece.

The many pieces of tableware packed for a trot around the globe, day trips to the country, or an extended journey across the Atlantic can now be used on our own tables to create settings that recall the days when whistles and foghorns beckoned, and when even confirmed homebodies took to the rails, roads, and the open sea in search of adventure.

**BELOW AND OPPOSITE:**
*Breakfast on deck with Foley easy-to-stack china, just right for packing into tight places. Christofle Ruban flatware and Elkington's cruet and salt and pepper shakers.*

All aboard! A mural
made from all the
different woods used on
the *Queen Mary* makes
a magnificent backdrop
for a lively card game.
A striking Bavarian tea
set from 1925, flatware
by Elkington, and an Art
Deco candlestick have
been set for guests who
like a little nourishment
while they play.

# People, Places, & Things

COLLECTIONS ARE VERY PERSONAL THINGS, BORN OUT OF AN INTRICATE SET OF LIKES AND DISLIKES THAT ARE A PART OF EVERY ONE OF US. WHETHER THEY FAVOR HOTEL SILVER, BONE CHINA, OR DELICATELY ETCHED GLASS, COLLECTORS ARE TRADITIONALLY VERY EXCLUSIVE IN THEIR TASTES—SEARCHING FOR THAT CERTAIN HOTEL NAME, THAT SPECIAL MAKER, OR A SPECIFIC COLOR VERY OFTEN MAKES THEM STRAY FROM THE BEATEN PATH IN ORDER TO TRACK DOWN A SOURCE NOT FOUND IN ANY ANTIQUES GUIDE. THE ATTACHMENT THAT PEOPLE DEVELOP FOR THEIR POSSESSIONS IS STRONG, AND LEADS MANY TO IMPRINT THEM WITH THEIR OWN ARTFULLY DESIGNED MONOGRAM OR FAMILY CREST. IN THIS CHAPTER WE WILL LEARN A LITTLE ABOUT THE PEOPLE, PLACES, AND THINGS THAT HAVE BEEN SO MUCH A PART OF THIS BOOK AND, WE HOPE, GAIN A NEW RESPECT FOR THE PEOPLE, PLACES, AND THINGS IN OUR OWN LIVES.

The words "Grand Hotel" evoke images of stately Beaux-Arts–style architecture inhabited by a well-mannered, appropriately dressed clientele. That most fascinating of actresses, Greta Garbo, stayed in just such a hotel, along with John and Lionel Barrymore and Joan Crawford, in the legendary 1932 film *Grand Hotel,* which captured on celluloid the busy comings and goings in a luxurious establishment that, although fictional, closely resembled many great hotels of that time.

The Ritz in Paris, The Carlton in London, and, of course, The Plaza in New York were to become bastions of good taste that promised all who entered their elegantly outfitted lobbies passage into a privileged world where they might rub elbows with a head of state or millionaire in one or another of the hotel's glamorous dining rooms. During the early part of the twentieth century, a number of grand hotels were built, and, for the most part, they met with great success by catering to the wealthy, like George Jay Gould and Mr. and Mrs. Alfred Gwynne Vanderbilt, who signed long-term leases at The Plaza for suites of rooms where they could live while their main residence was being refurbished. For the not-so-wealthy, eating a sumptuous dinner prepared by a great chef and served with the finest china, crystal, and silver that money could buy was reserved for celebrating life's special occasions.

The Savoy Hotel opened in London in 1889 and soon became a great success, in part due to some clever lighting; the restaurant of the hotel was lit with a soft, flattering glow meant to enhance the beauty of the lady customers. Because of this ingenious ruse, the female clientele grew rapidly, becoming faithful patrons. The Savoy Hotel still stands today, on one of the few streets in London that allow cars to be driven on the right side of the street; this exception to England's drive-on-the-left traffic rule stems from an order by the hotel's first manager, who so wanted to protect his lady customers' clothes and

**PRECEDING PAGES:** *Ebony, ivory, and mother-of-pearl have been used in exotic Indian furniture that delights the eye, and which is enhanced by a collection of serving pieces, small red-lacquer cups, and Grimwade's 1920s Rideau Ware with painted scenes in rich enamel colors.*

**OPPOSITE:** *A tall black pagoda is the focal point in an extraordinarily beautiful room. A Cauldon gold-and-white Art Deco tea set awaits guests.*

**RIGHT, BELOW, AND OPPOSITE:** *A fantasy lunch in Tony Duquette's private Shangri-la is served under a clear blue sky with Fornisetti green Malachite plates from 1940, classic 1910 French silver flatware with ivory handles, Moroccan water glasses, and abalone shells used for soup. Gold-flashed antique fawn and pagoda whiskey tumblers are also on the table. Tony's signature plaster sculptures form a practical centerpiece that is set on a cloth of his own design.*

*The chinoiserie-painted round breakfast room at Meadow Brook Hall is set for luncheon with Minton green-and-gold china, Mrs. Wilson's collection of jade cups and Chinese figures, yellow Venetian glass, and Rogers 1920 silver flatware.*

shoes in inclement weather that he instructed all cabs pulling up to the hotel to park directly in front of the hotel's entrance rather than across the street. In 1895 at The Savoy, a high-living group of young Englishmen who had just won 350,000 francs at the roulette tables in Monte Carlo threw themselves a celebration dinner, to be prepared by the famous chef Escoffier. Since their winning bet had been placed on red, the hotel staff paid homage to the "lucky" color with a table strewn with red roses, red menus, and red chairs (with the winning number, 9, posted on their backs); in addition, the entire banquet room was decorated with palm trees to evoke the Riviera, and these were strung with red lightbulbs.

The Algonquin Hotel, which opened in New York in 1902, presented itself as an apartment hotel, as did most of the era's great hotels, offering full restaurant services to residents and nonresidents. It set out to alleviate what one newspaper of the day called "the vexatious servant problem," by providing well-trained, courteous, efficient service to all who entered the premises. In addition to being one of the first hotels to cater to theatergoers and actors from the nearby theater district, The Algonquin was to become world-famous as a meeting place for some of the great wits and writers of the 1930s, who gathered in the hotel's dining room on a regular basis, always seated at the same table—eventually nicknamed The Algonquin Round Table.

At New York's Knickerbocker Hotel, which was built by John Jacob Astor in 1909, no expense was spared in making sure that the dining room was supplied with fine tableware; the hotel owned a solid-gold service for forty-

**OPPOSITE:** *Hollywood's fascination with chinoiserie in the 1920s and 1930s sets the mood for this setting by the pool. Aynsley 1930s hand-painted enamel luncheon plates, green-and-gold dinner plates by Black Knight, green Depression Glass iced-tea goblets, and various serving pieces and figures from the host's collection of Chinese "Faux Jade" and artifacts create an exotic and exciting dinner event.*

**ABOVE:** *Beautifully mono-grammed napkins and place-mats of linen and lace, like this splendid collection at the Ford House, were luxuri-ous accoutrements of elegant parties.*

eight as well as an abundance of Sèvres china, which was used for many memorable dinners. One such dinner saw the hotel's ballroom transformed into an Italianate garden, complete with gravel paths that wound their way through real sod that had been brought in especially for the occasion; vases and bronze figures contributed to the land-scape, where invited guests drank vintage 1838 champagne from gold-rimmed goblets, ate off gold plates, and were serenaded by the great opera singer Enrico Caruso. Every departing guest received a desk clock, which was embossed with his or her monogram.

Astor's other grand hotel, the St. Regis, was billed as a place where people could feel as comfortable as they did at home, and here, too, fine china—by Royal Worcester and Royal Minton—was on the "menu," as well as Royal Sèvres and a complete solid-gold flatware service. Such was the popularity of dining in style at hotel restaurants that, when the end of World War I was announced in London, with the signing of the armistice at 11 a.m. on November 11, 1918, every sin-

gle table at The Carlton Hotel was reserved for dinner by 1 p.m. and more than seven hundred meals had to be made at breakneck speed.

In addition to being places to see and be seen, hotels that were out of town, situated in the cool countryside or way up in the mountains, provided relief from the city's heat and offered families a chance to spend some time together swimming, boating, and letting go of the tensions accumulated during the year. While the rich had their "camps," great houses built in the Adirondacks that were supplied with all of the fineries the owners enjoyed in their city town houses, the rest of the population took great pleasure in spending their vacations at resorts like The Greenbrier in West Virginia, first opened in 1858, where one could take the waters, which promised to ease rheumatism and contribute to an overall state of

good health. Golf was one of the hotel's greatest allures and attracted players from across the country, including, in 1914, President Woodrow Wilson; upon the president's arrival, throngs of hotel guests came out to meet him at his private railroad car. Mr. and Mrs. Joseph P. Kennedy also arrived at The Greenbrier in 1914, for a two-week honeymoon following their October wedding in Boston. The hotel's guest register during the first two decades of the twentieth century read like a Who's Who of society—Pulitzer, Guggenheim, Bloomingdale, Carnegie, Rockefeller, Vanderbilt—but perhaps the most famous of all the visitors to The Greenbrier during this era was the Prince of Wales in 1919, later King Edward VIII of England, until his abdication from the throne in 1936 to marry Wallis

Warfield Simpson. With his party of thirty-five, the Prince of Wales occupied the entire third floor of the hotel.

For those who made up what was alternately called the "smart set" or "café society" during the 1920s, The Greenbrier provided an ideal spot to spend spring and autumn, since most guests traveled by rail between winter homes in Palm Beach, Florida, and summer homes at Newport, Rhode Island, Southampton, New York, or Bar Harbor, Maine. During the late 1920s, plans were drawn up to expand the hotel while taking great pains to preserve its Georgian character. Throughout the 1930s, the resort flourished with dinner balls, nightly movies, and polo and golf tournaments, which drew such famous golfers as Bing Crosby and Bob Hope. Unlike so many

of the country's earliest grand hotels, The Greenbrier has managed to survive and thrive. Guests today are served dinner on plates that are reproductions of President Andrew Jackson's White House china.

Today, the remnants of the fine tableware that once belonged to the grand hotels that have forever closed their doors, and the monogrammed silver and china that once set sail on great ships like the *Queen Mary,* are as carefully catalogued and sought after as sunken treasure; many collectors confine their search for pieces of hotel ware to one particular hotel. The hotel might appeal to them because it was featured in a favorite movie (The Carlton Hotel in Cannes was as much a star of Alfred Hitchcock's *To Catch a Thief* as was Cary Grant or Grace Kelly), or the hotel might have been where they spent their honeymoon—but whatever the reason, discovering a piece of china, silver, or glass bearing the name they are looking for is a thrill that justifies the many detours and dead ends that are so often a part of the hunt.

Just like the grand hotels that proudly put their names on their silver and china, a great many people put their family's crest or monogram on their tableware. A family's coat of arms or monogram was often engraved within a decorative cartouche in a prominent place on a piece of silver, particularly on larger objects. The style of the cartouche offers invaluable clues for dating pieces that lack a full set of silver marks. As for collecting such tableware today, there seem to be two schools of thought—one cherishes the monogram or coat of arms, which they see as personal, decorative touches connecting them to the original owners of the pieces, while the other feels that such markings devalue a piece, and they just do not like having a stranger's initials on pieces they want to use on their own table.

*Old Ivory china by the Syracuse China Company is referred to as "The Gold Service" and is still used for V.I.P. events at The Greenbrier. In one's own home, old hotel service plates would add distinction to any mix of patterns.*

**ABOVE AND RIGHT:**
*Hotel silver serving dishes
and coffee pots at the
ready.*

**OPPOSITE:** *Hotelware
silver serves up fabulous
desserts on a rolling pas-
try cart. Hotelwares were
durable, heavy-duty, and
often triple-plated to
withstand constant use
and cleaning.*

**OPPOSITE:** *Even a casual Sunday-night private screening of a favorite movie can feel like a premiere with Royal Worcester 1930 Arden pattern plates for snacks, an 1890 Ashworth bowl for popcorn, and etched hock glasses or polo tumblers for soft drinks or beer.*

**ABOVE:** *A cozy and glamorous room-service dinner for two aboard the* Queen Mary *is served on 1930s Rosenthal china. All of the silver is by Elkington, the etched glass is by Walter Dorwin Teague for Steuben, the conical glass is a "bottoms-up" martini glass from the Prohibition era, and in the background Marlene Dietrich (often a* Queen Mary *passenger) displays her famous legs in a photograph by Milton Greene, Joshua Greene's father, that appeared on the cover of* Life *magazine.*

Vintage silver trays are almost always engraved with a coat of arms or initials that decorate the center of the tray, which might appear somewhat plain without the traditional flourish of a monogram. For those purchasing old silver trays, soup tureens, gravy boats, and tankards or tumblers, it is good to know how to discern if a monogram, and so on, has been removed, since this can damage the piece by thinning the silver and creating a marked dip. A reliable method for detecting whether a piece has had a coat of arms or monogram removed (or replaced with a new one) is to check carefully whether there is an area that has oxidized differently from the rest of the piece; breathing heavily on a suspect area can also help to reveal erased or replaced monograms or crests.

Monogrammed table linens and napkins are charming, and since monogramming one's table accessories was so fashionable at the turn of the century and well up until the 1940s, there are many examples of monogrammed linens to choose from.

The people whom we are visiting in this book were all collectors; their many trips and holidays both abroad and in America yielded a bounty of objects that intrigue us today for their high level of craftsmanship and timeless beauty. Part of the pleasure of "hunting and gathering" is found in the sharing of one's collections with others; the dining table is the perfect place to show off and use the objects of our affections, and a party provides the perfect opportunity for doing just that.

Virginia Robinson, at her Beaux-Arts mansion in Beverly Hills, had her tables set with Baccarat glass and Limoges china for parties, and she instructed her servants to match the table linen to the partic-

**OPPOSITE AND ABOVE:**
*The ladies' dressing room at Van Dyke Place captures a scene from the past—Anna Thompson Dodge getting ready for one of her famous dinner parties, sipping wine from one of her prized Steuben glasses. The most expensive glasses made by Steuben in the 1920s were $238 a dozen! Family photos and pictures of her yacht, the* Delphine, *one of her haute couture Worth gowns, and a beaded evening bag help us envision life in the Roaring Twenties.*

ular gown she would be wearing that evening. Her place card (which she always had sent ahead to homes where she would be attending a dinner party) was her signature done in raised gold on porcelain by Tiffany; a specially made Lady Bell with which to call the servants was also made for her by Tiffany, and was given to her in honor of her fortieth birthday. Since she was an avid animal lover who almost never let her beloved dogs out of her sight, a Chinese porcelain foo dog was a most welcome table decoration. In the 1920s, in addition to the ongoing fascination with Japonisme an interest in the food and the decorative arts of China was born and hostesses often decorated their tables with Chinese figurines when their menu featured Western adaptations of dishes imported from that country.

Objects that have been collected over a lifetime, be they simple souvenirs from favorite vacations or mementos passed along from a relative, narrate a personal history that is to many more valuable than the finest antique with the lengthiest provenance and the highest price tag. In his novel *Madame Bovary,* Gustave Flaubert describes a doctor's wonder at his young wife's collecting habit, marveling that one day "she wanted two large vases of blue glass on her fireplace and, a while later, an ivory work box with a vermeil thimble." Although he does not fully understand her passion for accumulating pretty objects for the house, he finds that "they added something to his sensual pleasures and to the sweetness of his home as if gold dust were being spread all along the narrow path of his life."

# Meet Me at the Bar

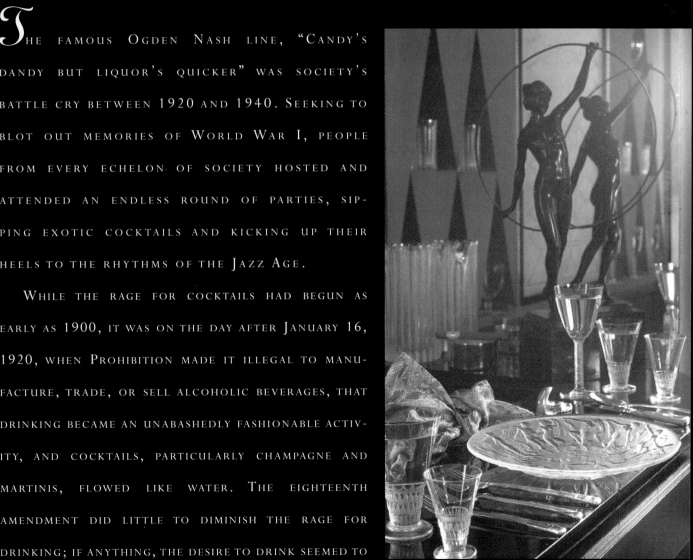

THE FAMOUS OGDEN NASH LINE, "CANDY'S DANDY BUT LIQUOR'S QUICKER" WAS SOCIETY'S BATTLE CRY BETWEEN 1920 AND 1940. SEEKING TO BLOT OUT MEMORIES OF WORLD WAR I, PEOPLE FROM EVERY ECHELON OF SOCIETY HOSTED AND ATTENDED AN ENDLESS ROUND OF PARTIES, SIPPING EXOTIC COCKTAILS AND KICKING UP THEIR HEELS TO THE RHYTHMS OF THE JAZZ AGE.

WHILE THE RAGE FOR COCKTAILS HAD BEGUN AS EARLY AS 1900, IT WAS ON THE DAY AFTER JANUARY 16, 1920, WHEN PROHIBITION MADE IT ILLEGAL TO MANUFACTURE, TRADE, OR SELL ALCOHOLIC BEVERAGES, THAT DRINKING BECAME AN UNABASHEDLY FASHIONABLE ACTIVITY, AND COCKTAILS, PARTICULARLY CHAMPAGNE AND MARTINIS, FLOWED LIKE WATER. THE EIGHTEENTH AMENDMENT DID LITTLE TO DIMINISH THE RAGE FOR DRINKING; IF ANYTHING, THE DESIRE TO DRINK SEEMED TO

multiply many times over after it became forbidden to do so. It must be acknowledged that nowhere did it state in the amendment that it was illegal to drink alcohol, only that it was against the law to sell it, and that was probably why Prohibition was doomed from the start—the joyous spirit of the Roaring Twenties wouldn't be dampened and people balked at packing away their shakers and swizzle sticks. The day after the amendment was passed, the 50-50 Club opened over a New York City garage, selling bootlegged whiskey.

The cocktail party replaced the tea dance, and even the hour of the evening meal was put back, worldwide and in America, for the evening hour of the drink. When Wall Street began to totter in 1929, leading to what would become the Great Depression, many people in Europe and

America virtually lived for the cocktail hour, when anxieties could be drowned in an extra-dry martini or a double Scotch. Elaborately prepared libations were served with great panache on trays of reflective colored glass with silver or chrome trims by tuxedo-clad waiters at ritzy affairs, or by young housewives closely adhering to the advice of the high priestess of etiquette, Emily Post, on how to host the perfect soirée. Top glass and silver designers fueled the endless round of swank cocktail parties with glasses, decanters, cocktail shakers, canapé trays, and serving bowls.

Fashionable home bars, like the one installed in 1927 by James Oviatt in his penthouse topping the towering Los Angeles building bearing his name, featured fine glass. Actually, the Oviatt Building held the single largest display of Lalique glass outside France, for Oviatt had commissioned the famous French designer not only to create his bar but also to outfit the men's clothing store he operated on the two ground floors of

the building, one of California's first skyscrapers. The bar was wood dazzlingly carved and polished into fashionable Deco points and streamlined curves, and Oviatt could reach for Lalique wineglasses, tumblers, and champagne flutes, and regale his guests with a well-mixed cocktail.

Edsel and Eleanor Ford installed a bar composed entirely of African woods in the ultramodern Art Deco room of their mansion in Grosse Pointe, Michigan, which featured work by African-American artists who depicted scenes of African life. Thoughtful hosts eager to accommodate teetotalers employed an ingenious two-faced bar on

OPPOSITE: *Displayed at the Saarinen House, Art Deco barware includes a martini shaker in a black-and-silver linear design from their collection and a matching glass and decanter set. The fireplace surround is a Saarinen design executed by Detroit's Pewabic Tile Company under the personal supervision of owner Mary Chase Perry Stratton. Orrefors black smoky glasses complement the practical movable bar designed by Eliel Saarinen.*

LEFT: *A sterling-silver martini shaker with silver cocktail glasses and tray reflect the impact of modern architectural design, especially in barwares. The mirrored alcove served as a bar in the Teague-designed Modern Room at the Ford House.*

wheels, designed by Eliel Saarinen, which featured one side for mixing alcoholic drinks and one side for preparing nonalcoholic drinks.

Although the engraved glass that was the height of fashion at the end of the nineteenth century was still made and loved well into the 1920s, the public yearned to look as chic as their favorite celebrities did. To satisfy the yearning for glasses and cocktail shakers that would create a Hollywood ambience even within the many conservatively designed houses that were popping up along the outskirts of the big cities across America, fashionable Deco glassware gradually edged out the more traditional styles. In Prague, during the 1920s, the Czechs contributed beautiful designs that would make them world-famous and highly respected as premier glass makers.

Top designers, like Baccarat, made striking, chunky glasses that were often accompanied by angular decanters decorated with black-enamel transfer prints. The penchant for using glasses with the same pattern but in different colors created an informal harlequin look that projected a jaunty air just right for the times; this attitude still exists today as collectors of cocktail-era memorabilia set up their own home bars, mixing and matching delightfully whimsically shaped glasses and cocktail shakers. While gay Depression Glass colors like pale pink, green, amber, and blue filled middle-class homes in the twenties and thirties, there was a good

**RIGHT:** *A French café glass advertising Stella Artois, which has long been the bistro glass of choice.*

**BELOW:** *Swinging a solid "gate" on the 88s, these ebony and silver diamond-patterned cordial glasses are very Moderne.*

deal of smoky-black glass as well, often juxtaposed with bands of red, made by companies like Fostoria and Tiffin, and a taste for decorated clear glass with modern excised decoration also found favor.

In wealthy households, platters of savory appetizers and generous bowls of beluga caviar were arranged in the butler's pantry on fine silver trays for chic cocktail parties that might include some of the leading industrialists of the day, discussing the distressing state of the economy or the progress being made in time management and worker efficiency.

The ritual of preparing and drinking fancy drinks was the foundation of the cocktail culture that sprang to life on the heels of Prohibition, and *The Savoy Cocktail Book* (1930), with its detailed instructions for making the most popular concoctions, became a bestseller that was purchased by barmen at speakeasies and suburban husbands alike. Women bought cocktail dresses and cocktail hats, with matching shoes and handbags, so they would be fashionably dressed for nights out at cocktail parties or at hotel ballrooms.

At cocktail parties in the 1920s, the Ouija board was often taken out and carefully studied by guests hoping to find the answers to all of life's problems, or well-traveled hosts shared the vacation photographs they took with their new Kodak Brownie cameras. Long glass swizzle sticks for stirring cocktails were mass-produced and often topped with novelty figures that reflected individual hobbies or careers.

Sometimes, a light supper, an after-theater snack, or a tray of dainty savories was served directly at the bar on glass plates, perhaps with a delicate, long silver olive fork at the ready to pluck a cocktail onion or an anchovy from a pretty cut-glass bowl. By 1922, both men and women

**ABOVE:** *Tropical motifs that conjured up sun-drenched islands and tropical drinks were fashionable during the 1930s.*

**LEFT:** *Strictly modern, an interplay of red and black, a favorite Art Deco color combination, is used on an assortment of Czechoslovakian barwares and decorative black-satin glasswares by Tiffin.*

smoked publicly, and a pretty glass tumbler was often placed right on the bar to hold cigarettes, as were a few heavy cut-glass ashtrays.

Before the turn of the century, decanter sets often included no less than eighty-seven pieces, including twelve glasses each for sherry, port, claret, and champagne, but by the 1920s and into the 1930s the number of glasses had dwindled sharply. Whiskey sets had six shot glasses with a matching decanter and water jug, while cocktail sets had the all-important shaker, most often used for preparing martinis, or "silver bullets," as they were often called; lemonade, lager, and water sets consisted of tall, usually straight-sided jugs and half-pint tumblers.

Decanters often were bell-shaped with bold stoppers; cordials, such as crème de menthe, were served in cordial glasses, which were often cobalt blue. Steuben pioneered glassware decorated with metallic enamels, wedges or bands of black; their colored enamels, combined with transfer prints of polka dots, colored stripes, and renditions of jazzy dancers, brought a dash of sophisticated Deco glamour to middle-class homes. At Steuben, Frederick Carder made glasses with rhythmic curves and zigzags that were reminiscent of the Chrysler Building's towering spire.

During the heyday of the cocktail, the Bloody Mary, Side Car, Gin Fizz, Tom Collins, Manhattan, and dozens of other drinks were concocted. By the 1920s, an indication that Hollywood's fantasy celluloid world was spilling over into everyday life became apparent in the number of cocktails being named after silent-screen

**OPPOSITE:** *Every well-made martini needs an olive and a beautiful fork with which to pluck it from a bowl. Here is an assortment of olive forks and spoons and a small Robert Jarvie silver bowl from 1910 with an Indian motif.*

**LEFT:** *A "Thirst Extinguisher" martini shaker from the 1930s.*

**ABOVE:** *M is for martini on this shaker by Heisey. The martini glass at left is by Frederick Carder for Steuben. The tall glass is Riedel. Allan Adler designed the silver and glass candlesticks in 1939.*

ABOVE: *A variety of turquoise-tint glasses with fantasy stems of the 1930s made by Bryce Brothers, West Virginia, look just right for a drink at the bar on the* Queen Mary.

OPPOSITE, ABOVE: *This Cambridge square-bottom decanter and matching glasses on a hotelware tray add Art Deco style to room service.*

OPPOSITE, BELOW: *These Baccarat etched decanters in bell shapes with bold stoppers were made in France in the 1920s, and are one collector's recent find.*

stars. The Mary Pickford, for example, was a razzle-dazzle blend of pineapple juice, rum, and grenadine. Within movie houses, newsreels often showed stars relaxing at home, cocktail in hand, or hosting parties with free-flowing champagne poured into beautiful conical martini glasses balancing precariously on pencil-thin stems. Nothing was more Hollywood than shaking up a batch of fresh martinis in a gleaming silver cocktail shaker and having a bottle of French champagne chilling in a silver ice bucket in preparation for a toast to a newlywed couple, or perhaps, to wish Charles Lindbergh good luck on his historic flight across the Atlantic in May 1927.

Many believed that Prohibition came about as the result of vociferous advocates of temperance in the women's suffrage movement, which was at its peak in 1918, but nothing could be further from the truth, for many women actually emerged as the cocktail culture's greatest fans. After being banned for so many years from Victorian drinking rituals, women flocked to speakeasies to enjoy the gaiety of the clandestinely chic establishments. Prohibition was the result of vociferous temperance leaders, like Carrie Nation, who spent their considerable energies on a narrowly focused agenda that pressured politicians into making every state "dry."

American ingenuity knew no bounds when it came to outwitting the enforcers of the unpopular amendment, and even establishments like the sophisticated 21 Club in New York devised sneaky maneuvers to foil police raids; the club had an emergency button that, when pressed, would automatically flip the bottles on the bar shelf down a chute to the basement. So-called Bottoms Up martini glasses had no stems and could be quickly turned over in case of a raid. A well-known theater critic of the 1920s, George Jean Nathan, was reputed to have an ingenious device rigged to his front door that set a cocktail shaker in the refrigerator in motion as soon as he turned the key to enter his home, so that a martini was ready for him by the time he reached the kitchen.

More than any other drink, the martini was *the* drink of the 1920s and 1930s; after being shaken, *not* stirred, the drink was either ceremoniously poured into glasses or into a tall, slim pitcher that would serve a number of people. Some companies listed the ingredients for the perfect martini on their shakers while others, like Heisey, etched a large *M* into the glass to define the vessel's purpose. President Franklin Delano Roosevelt delighted in mixing extra-dry martinis for himself and visiting dignitaries at the White House. After a visit to the nation's capital, the playwright and actor Noël Coward described FDR's desk being cleared of paperwork and "littered with an elaborate paraphernalia of cocktail implements. There were bottles, glasses of different sizes for short and long drinks, dishes of olives and nuts and cheese straws, also an ice

bucket, a plate of lemons with a squeezer, a bowl of brown sugar, two kinds of bitters and an imposing silver shaker."

The cocktail shaker was a new invention, designed not only to shake the drink mixture it contained but also to strain out fruit while pouring. Designers let their imaginations run wild when it came to cocktail shakers, many of which resembled skyscrapers; today, a collection of these, interspersed with martini glasses and champagne flutes, would create a miniature Manhattan skyline when lined up along a shelf behind the bar. In addition to sleek cocktail shakers of glass, chrome, or silver, demand grew for ice buckets to hold cubed, shaved, or crushed ice; many of these featured clear glass liners to keep bottles chilled and, to this day, a silver ice bucket is a traditional wedding or silver-anniversary gift.

With the repeal of Prohibition in 1933, Americans could once again imbibe out in the light of the sun, and were no longer required to utter secret passwords to gain entry into speakeasies or to drink harsh, homemade "bathtub gin." At this time, a London exhibition of Swedish glass featured the simple, understated engraved designs of the Orrefors glass factory, which often decorated its pieces on both sides to produce a delightful three-dimensional effect. The sophisticated designs were a hit, and, in America, Steuben adapted the sparse, uncluttered look of Orrefors to the American market, using motifs on its glassware very similar to those being incorporated onto china at the time—figures in athletic poses, mythological notables like Zeus, and classical scenes that captured the flavor of ancient Greece. Steuben also developed a range of crystal ware that incorporated elongated, sleek, highly stylized animals, crisply engraved to give the impression of bas-relief. Interestingly, Walter Dorwin Teague worked for Steuben for a short period following 1932, and his clear glass blown and engraved stemware, much like his furniture and industrial designs, was both elegant and functional.

Fostoria, as part of a huge advertising campaign in the early 1930s, aimed at housewives stocking their new built-in bars, bowed to the interest in astronomy that prevailed at the time. The glass manufacturer gave away horoscope/zodiac flyers at department-store counters that, in addition to telling one's future, included an unusual drink recipe and the particular glass pattern that would be just right for serving the concoction and toasting "Here's mud in your eye!" Fostoria's free "Guide to How to Use Your Crystal" listed some of the more popular glass sizes and shapes, with suggestions for alternative uses: 16-ounce magnums, while traditionally used for hearty red wines, could be used for mixed drinks, fruit

**OPPOSITE:** *Here are Lalique's Roxanne decanter filled with crème de menthe and Golf Ball cobalt cordial glasses by Morgantown.*

**ABOVE:** *Spirals of glass increasing in size form a martini glass that is very Moderne in style.*

juices, or seafood cocktails; both large and small claret glasses might be used for serving liqueur over ice; 10-ounce goblets were suitable for both water and wine; 6-ounce champagne or Continental champagne flutes, while perfect for champagne, of course, could double as servers for seafood cocktails; 13-ounce double old-fashioned and highball glasses were fine for beer or iced tea; 6-ounce stemmed cocktail glasses made for holding cocktails straight up would be equally suitable for holding after-dinner drinks; and a 15-ounce brandy inhaler, traditionally cradled in the palm of the hand to warm the spirits within it, was recommended as a creative serving dish for a fancy layered dessert like trifle or for a few generous scoops of sherbet or ice cream.

For those who had disdained alcoholic beverages before, during, and after Prohibition, hotels like The Greenbrier, as well as fine restaurants and, indeed, any well-mannered host, served lemonade in pitcher and glass sets of frosted glass, often decorated with swaying palm trees that sought to capture some of the tropical flavor of California and Florida. For those desiring nothing stronger than a pot of black coffee, a breakfast set was graciously placed directly on the bar, with an elegant silver cake stand heaped with delicate, sugary sweets so that nobody would be left out of the fun.

While a great amount of attention is usually focused on art glass or on glass that was specifically manufactured for integration with interior design projects of the early 1900s and of the 1920s and 1930s, it is the table glass that is most within the grasp of collectors today. The spirited barware made for the roaring twenties and glamorous thirties is still wholeheartedly welcomed at cocktail parties today, where the glass happily blends with contemporary designs for events that are absolutely "the snake's hips."

*Coffee or tea is served before an amusing mural at The Greenbrier, using a proper Edwardian breakfast set and a three-tier silver stand with sweets for a late-afternoon pickup that mixes moods and periods with charm.*

# DINNER AT EIGHT

THE GLAMOROUS GOWNS, TUXEDOS, MODERNE SETS, AND CLEVER ON-SCREEN REPARTEE WERE ALL PART OF MGM's 1933 FILM CLASSIC *DINNER AT EIGHT*, WITH JEAN HARLOW AND JOHN BARRY- MORE CREATING A FANTASY WORLD FAR REMOVED FROM THE REALITIES JUST OUTSIDE THE MOVIE THEATER'S DOORS, WHERE MEN SOLD APPLES FOR A FEW CENTS APIECE OR LINED UP IN THE DEMORALIZING BREADLINES THAT WERE PART OF THE GREAT DEPRESSION. THE GREAT COMMERCIAL SUCCESS OF THE FILM ATTESTED TO THE FACT THAT THE MOVIES WERE A SIGNIFI- CANT AVENUE OF ESCAPE FROM THE ANXIETIES THAT MARKED DAILY EXISTENCE FOR SO MANY AFTER THE STOCK MARKET CRASHED IN 1929. THE AUDIENCE COULD GAZE UP AT THE SILVER SCREEN AND SEE FAVORITE STARS ENGAGED IN CLEVERLY WRITTEN DIALOGUE WITH CHEERFUL, CAREFREE GUESTS GATHERED FOR A SMART COCKTAIL PARTY OR A SPARKLING DINNER TABLE.

**PRECEDING PAGES:**

*Timeless modernity captures the twilight moment for an extravagant dinner party featuring china designed by Frank Lloyd Wright, Lalique frosted glass, and Gorham's Etruscan flatware from 1923. Steuben ombre-cobalt finger bowls coordinate with cobalt-blue 1930s champagne glasses by Morgantown. The host sets his own style by placing all of the flatware to the left and napkins to the right of the dinner plates.*

**OPPOSITE AND BELOW:**

*French doors, left ajar, welcome guests to dinner on the terrace. On the table are Coalport 1920 pink-and-gold dinner plates, 1890 Hammersley hand-painted dessert plates signed by Marpie, San Lorenzo silver flatware introduced in 1916 by Tiffany, and Venetian hand-blown glasses decorated with camellias. The matching candelabra and centerpiece holds the pink camellia that was named for Virginia Robinson.*

An empty table is like a blank canvas awaiting the touch of the painter's brush: with an artistic eye and a bit of imagination, a creative host or hostess fills a table with subtle or striking dabs of color by assembling treasured pieces of tinted glass; orchestrates interesting pockets of texture by cradling the smoothest silver in linen napkins; skillfully weaves an intriguing assortment of shapes, perhaps a favorite small sculpture or set of carved candlesticks, into the landscape; and, finally, stands back and admires the shining result. Premier hostesses, like Virginia Robinson and Anna Thompson Dodge, often spent days supervising the setting of their tables with hundreds of pieces from their fabled tableware collections. Each wanted, in her own inimitable way, to delight the guests who had come to her home to share a cocktail, a meal, and an evening of good conversation—and what better way to delight them than with a table laden with beautiful things?

In Virginia Robinson's Beaux-Arts mansion, a dinner party would have presented the ideal opportunity to display some of the treasures gathered on the many European trips the Robinsons had taken during their life together. A sophisticated blending of china, glass, and silver might have paid homage to two of Mrs. Robinson's favorite things: the color pink and the camellia (a *Camellia japonica* would eventually be named for her, in 1957, by Nuccio's Nursery in California). Pink-and-gold china by Coalport, gently set aglow by the light of candles in a Venetian-glass candelabra, would have looked stunning set off with fine silver flatware for a dinner to which particularly good friends had been invited. Elegant Venetian wineglasses featuring camellias abloom on their stems might have been filled with an Italian wine to toast the health of the assembled guests, and dessert might have been presented on Hammersley plates made in 1890 that featured paintings of some of the birds that were regularly spotted in the hostess's lush gardens.

Mrs. Robinson, who was fondly known as the First Lady of Beverly Hills during her sixty-six-year "reign" of the town, which began in 1911, was hostess to such luminaries as Charlie Chaplin, Clark Gable, Mary Pickford, Amelia Earhart, and the Duke and Duchess of Windsor (the Duchess had once asserted that if one accepts a dinner invitation, one has "a moral obligation to be amusing").

For a dinner like the ones Mrs. Robinson often had, a hostess today might choose to keep the mood very Beverly Hills with fronds from the city's ubiquitous palm trees used as place mats; damask napkins and nineteenth-century wineglasses the color of the Pacific; Academy Award–gold Moroccan-style embossed dinner plates; and some fine Limoges and heirloom silver. Another inventive hostess of the day, Mrs. Eliel Saarinen, often chose pineapple upside-down cake to serve for dessert at her dinner parties because its warm yellow matched the color of her dining room. Such a quirk is not as idiosyncratic as it might sound—today, many tabletop stylists working for fashionable department stores or home-decorating magazines often pick up the colors used within a room or featured on a model when they set a table, because the color harmony thus achieved is particularly pleasing to the eye.

In French-inspired town houses like Van Dyke Place in Detroit, built at the turn of the century by the businessman/philanthropist William Muir Finck, dinner might have been served on an ormolu-edged mahogany table graced with pale green Bavarian china, embossed with gold bands and a filigree overlay, befitting a captain of industry and his family. Guests who had seen their host's house (which contained an unexpected series of beautifully designed Arts and Crafts–style rooms in the basement) in the pages of *Town & Country* magazine in 1912, where it was featured as "House of the Year," probably would have requested a thorough house tour after finishing that last cup of coffee.

While there are many similarities between today's tables and those set during the early years of the twentieth century, and certainly during the

OPPOSITE: *This jewel-box dining room is the dramatic setting for a mélange of the owner's gilded-lacquer tablewares. The orange-and-gold china is an asymmetrical design by Dorothy Thorpe, as are the tall fluted water goblets and wineglasses that are diffused with gold flashing. The flatware has lovely mother-of-pearl handles.*

1920s and 1930s, the means and methods by which dinner was presented to one's guests changed dramatically after the Victorian era, which formally ended with Victoria's death in 1901. A Victorian host or hostess mailed (or had a servant hand-deliver) written invitations to guests, who were then expected to reply in kind in a timely manner. The Victorian dinner party usually included six to ten diners, never thirteen (because of superstition); on the evening of the party, guests took their seats, specially marked for them with beautifully printed place cards positioned above their dinner plates. A flower centerpiece, often featuring mosses and ferns, graced the table, which would have been dressed in white damask, awaiting a series of courses (usually at least ten), followed by finger bowls for a bit of dainty washing up and, at last, a serving of fruit, dessert, and cups of hot coffee.

A properly set Victorian table groaned under the weight of pounds of forks, spoons, and knives provided for everything from scooping oysters from their shells to cutting into some well-prepared turtle meat; the Victorians' abhorrence for actually having to touch food led to an alarmingly large number of utensils that were specially designed to prevent an egregious faux pas, like picking up a pickle with one's fingers. The formal Victorian dinner called for lots of dishes—dinner and dessert plates; soup bowls; dishes for salt, bones, and vegetables; platters; casserole dishes; gravy boats; berry bowls; and trays, pitchers, and compote dishes were regularly used. The great variety of mostly molded, pressed glass would have included wineglasses, goblets, celery vases, punch bowls, cake stands, salt and pepper shakers, sugar shakers, castor bottles, and a decanter, among various other pieces.

By the end of the nineteenth century, as a result of changes in society's codes of etiquette and diet, and, no doubt, by William Morris's pleas for simplification in home decoration, obvious attempts to display social status were considered to be in questionable taste, and the lavishly set tables that had been the norm for so many years gave way to simpler ones that stressed quality over quantity. By Edwardian times the fashionable dinner table had been noticeably thinned out. Lady Jeune, a well-known society hostess of the period, believed that "No dinner should consist of more than eight dishes—soup, fish, entrée, joint, game, sweet, hors d'oeuvre, and perhaps an ice." The invention of today's ubiquitous hors d'oeuvres can be traced to some clever late-nineteenth-century hotel and restaurant managers who saw them as a convenient way of amusing patrons awaiting their often slowly delivered dinner.

**OPPOSITE AND BELOW:**
*Dinner at eight with a Chinese character. Carleton's 1925 gold-embossed china features an enamel, hand-painted Oriental scene. Elegant cobalt water glasses mix with new tall twist-stem wines, and French 1910 faceted wines by St. Louis, gold salt and pepper shakers made in 1880 by Tiffany, and all are in a Beaux-Arts dining room resplendent with an 1890 Baccarat three-tier chandelier and mirrored tableau centerpiece.*

While the Arts and Crafts Movement can be credited for its part in spurring the weeding out of overcrowded, overdecorated rooms and tables, there was another indisputable and very practical reason for cutting down on the number of pieces laid upon the table—without servants, arranging (and polishing and washing up) so much tableware was almost impossible for many women.

The patterned, colored glass that was in such vogue during Victoria's long reign had begun to be replaced by opaque and satin art glass, with such intriguing names as Peachblow, Amberina, or Burmese by the 1880s, and L. C. Tiffany's iridescent gold, blue, and purple Favrile tulip-shaped glasses were considered the pièce de résistance by fashionable ladies who regularly shopped at the finest stores. In 1910, dinner in a middle-class household might be served on a handsome Stickley table crisscrossed with hand-embroidered runners and laid with colorful, gracefully shaped and etched glasses, probably no more than two sizes per setting, and dinner, salad, and dessert plates as well as coffee cups and saucers in a sophisticated yet simple pattern.

Another influence on the way tables were set between the two world wars was the peerless arbiter of what would one day come to be called lifestyle—Elsie de Wolfe. One of the world's very first interior decorators and a remarkably talented promoter, who was gifted with a natural sense for marketing, Elsie de Wolfe can be credited with teaching scores of women through her 1913 book, *The House in Good Taste,* how to create a comfortably chic home with a few yards of chintz and reproductions of fancy English and French eighteenth-century furniture. She was dubbed "The Chintz Lady," and her fondness for the fabric certainly was a factor in the period's love affair with Chintz ware; women must have reveled in the fact that they could create the ultimate Elsie de Wolfe room by serving dinner on plates that nearly perfectly matched their stylish new chintz dining-room curtains. In 1934, de Wolfe's new book, *Recipes for Successful Dining,* gave pointers for setting ravishing tables with gold

**OPPOSITE:** *A tall Murano glass from the 1930s, enamel-painted glass plates and tumblers made in 1925 Deco style by Delvaux would be perfect for an intimate "come for dessert" event.*

lamé, as well as giving readers a selection of essays on how to be a "brilliant hostess." She advised readers to follow her own practice of creating a cross-referenced "Dinner Party" filing system, detailing the guests, menu, and table setting of every dinner party given at one's house; such attention to detail would presumably prevent a hostess from ever committing the "sin" of repetition and help to sustain her reputation of always being fresh and innovative in her presentations.

Elsie de Wolfe had few hard-and-fast rules except these: "Plates should be hot, hot, hot; glasses cold, cold, cold; and table decorations low, low, low," and she firmly dictated to her guests that they should arrive on time for cocktails at 7:45 p.m. followed by dinner at eight. She was one of the first dinner hostesses to treat her guests to in-home movies shown on a projection screen set up in her living room, and it is probably safe to assume that *Dinner at Eight* was a favorite feature. She advised women to be creative in choosing the best place for their parties; she, herself, was fond of throwing parties at a Horn and Hardart Automat (with the tables set with her own china and linens, of course).

One of society's most highly respected authorities on good manners, Emily Post, conceded by the 1920s that "no rule of etiquette is less important than which fork we use." In 1932, the Gorham silver sales manual instructed salespeople to suggest various ways that individual pieces of hollowware could be used; in addition, representatives from many silver companies regularly visited department stores to give free seminars called "How to Set a Table." Tiffany & Co. in recent years has sponsored celebrity table settings, held at their stores to show women the many ways their silver can be used. Well-known people in theater, art, and music personally set tables that show the creative or playful side of their personalities. In the 1930s, after-dinner games like Twenty Questions and Charades were popular and legend has it that Elsie de Wolfe introduced the parlor murder game that became the rage at chic Thirties dinner parties and is still played today in a variety of forms.

By 1940, dinner-party menus almost always had a decidedly French accent, with soups like vichyssoise and delicacies like crêpes suzette showing up with great frequency on fashionable tables around town. Americans, who had been introduced to authentic Italian, Chinese, Cuban, and Swiss food at the 1939 World's Fair, probably sampled quite a bit of French food, as well, at the fair's Le Restaurant du Pavillon de France, and came home full of ideas for creating a memorable dinner party.

For those of us today who are privileged to live in a historical home, the desire to decorate a table completely in sync with the period of the house must be a strong one; and, yet, what fun it

would be to mix and match periods, using the walls and architectural details of the house as a splendid backdrop to a table set with pieces from a variety of eras. An asymmetrical orange-and-gold dinner set by the 1930s designer Dorothy Thorpe, and her tall, fluted gold-flashed water goblets would add a bit of Hollywood pizzazz to even a no-nonsense turn-of-the-century home, with not even one flapper or starlet in its long history of occupants.

While Edsel and Eleanor Ford hosted dinner parties for world-renowned guests, with four children, dinner at their house was, most often, a family affair. In their Cotswold-style mansion, the Fords' china included various sets of service plates of English and French manufacture, as well as many pieces of Chinese export porcelain; the butler's pantry, which adjoined the dining room, contained a series of glass-fronted cabinets that provided storage space for all of the tableware, linen, and flatware needed for a large, socially active family with many guests to entertain. The focal point of any meal would have been the Fords' Queen Anne–style dining table, which seated eighteen comfortably, and which, since there was no chandelier in the dining room, was always illuminated either by natural light, by candlelight from the candelabra and wall sconces, or by the light shed by the large fireplace that stood in the room. As a couple, the Fords always sat side by side facing the fire when not in the company of the many fascinating people that were often invited for dinner. Mrs. Ford, who had very refined taste, was quite adept at mixing periods when setting a table, and her creative flair was admired by her guests.

At the dinner parties in the Christopher Wren dining room at

*Color-flashed medallion glasses made in 1910 work splendidly with Royal Worcester's blue-and-yellow patterned 1920s botanical plates and Tiffany's Art Nouveau silver pattern Audubon, the first American pattern to be made in the Japanese Revival style. The sunny color combination brings contemporary style to the hand-painted linens, flowers, and candleshades.*

Meadow Brook Hall, Matilda Dodge Wilson's choice of tableware was traditional. For her parties, she was fond of using flowers from the huge grounds of the great estate to make stunning centerpieces.

To host a dinner party is to take part in a ritual. The new bride anxiously sets her brand-new wedding china and silverware for her very first dinner as mistress of her own home. The seasoned hostess sets a table that she has never arranged before with a wonderful set of china and an antique Venetian-glass candelabra she just bought at auction, and feels the excitement she experienced when she set her very first party table many years before. The satisfaction of designing a beautiful table for friends or family can be shared by anyone, and while one needn't be an heiress or a great decorator to host a memorable dinner party, the value of studying the tables of some of the century's most admired hostesses is immeasurable. The pure delight that comes from dining with antique tableware is one that should never be restricted to special occasions; every day should be enriched by its beauty and history.

# Home
## *for the* Holidays

**F**OR MOST OF US, HOLIDAYS ARE LIKE PUNCTUATION POINTS THAT ARE SCATTERED THROUGHOUT THE DAYS OF THE YEAR, MAKING US STOP, LOOK AROUND, AND TAKE SPECIAL NOTICE OF FAMILY AND FRIENDS BEFORE WE HURRY OFF TO THE NEXT CHAPTER IN THE ONGOING SAGA OF OUR LIVES. GOOD FOOD AND DRINK, LIKE LAUGHTER, SONG, AND PRETTY PACKAGES TIED UP WITH RIBBON, SEEM TO BE SYNONYMOUS WITH MEMORABLE HOLIDAY CELEBRATIONS, AND SETTING TABLES THAT CAPTURE THE EXCITEMENT OF CHRISTMAS EVE, THANKSGIVING DAY, OR A SPECIAL BIRTHDAY IS AT ONCE A CHALLENGE AND A DELIGHT.

WHILE IT IS TRUE THAT MOST HOLIDAYS COME COLOR-COORDINATED—SAINT VALENTINE'S DAY BEING RED; EASTER, THE PALEST SHADES OF LILAC AND YELLOW; THANKSGIVING, ORANGE, BROWN, AND YELLOW; AND CHRISTMAS, RED AND GREEN—SAVVY HOSTESSES KNOW THE PLEASURE TO BE FOUND

PRECEDING PAGES:
*Valentine's Day means red and romance and dinner in the music room at Van Dyke Place. The entire Venetian glass service of dinner plates and stemware is embellished with enameled cupids, and was once owned by a founding partner of the Chrysler Corporation. The 1936 King Edward flatware by Gorham was named for Edward VIII, who abdicated "For the woman I love."*

ABOVE: *A flower-handled tea set, hand-painted in Easter yellow and lilac adds a touch of whimsy to a holiday breakfast at The Greenbrier.*

in mixing things up a bit and poking a little fun at convention. It may be argued that for a table to be truly spectacular, it must be placed within a truly spectacular setting, such as the dining room at Van Dyke Place in Detroit, where bucolic scenes painted in oil surround diners as they raise a rosy glass in Santa Claus's or Cupid's honor, or the dining room of the Whitney House, where cornucopias are beautifully carved into the woodwork—and yet, a thoughtfully planned table, lovingly set with treasured heirlooms, is very much a world unto itself, much like a stage set, conjuring up an exotic ambience that transcends even the plainest environs.

Past eras come to life when vintage tableware is pressed into service, enabling us briefly to escape to a more genteel time when men tipped their hats to the ladies and children were instructed in the art of proper table manners. It is great fun to search for holiday motifs on tableware and, luckily, there is an abundance of turkeys, evergreens, rabbits, cherubs, and reindeer to be found on tableware made between 1890 and 1940. Pinecones were particularly popular during the Arts and Crafts period; they were often used on footed silver stands and flatware, and would be particularly appropriate today on a table set for a big Thanksgiving dinner. At Cranbrook, where so much Arts and Crafts silver was produced and used, there was a large array of silver hollowware that might have doubled as receptacles for fall bouquets put together with foliage grown in the famous Cranbrook gardens.

Much of the barware made during the 1930s featured cheery holiday figures such as leprechauns, elves, and prancing reindeer. Georg Jensen produced a 155-piece silver table service featuring an acorn pattern and magnificent caviar bowls mounted on pinecone-shaped feet; Spode made china that was whimsically hand-painted with turkeys and other game fowl; and Gorham produced silver soup tureens featuring reindeer. Depression Glass, in its myriad shades, offers an almost endless number of color combinations for holiday entertaining and looks especially striking when mixed with contemporary white china. It is interesting to note that Charles Rennie Mackintosh and his wife, Margaret McDonald, discovered the splendors of decorating with white in the early days of the twentieth century, aware of white's ability to make other colors pop when placed in juxtaposition to it.

A linen room, a wrapping closet, and a flower room equipped with professional floral refrigerators were considered essentials for Matilda Dodge Wilson, whose love of parties was matched only by her commitment to community service; a "modern woman" who was ahead of her time, she managed to raise four children, handle the family finances, take part in various clubs, head the National Council of Women during the late 1920s, and serve as chair of the board of Fidelity Bank and Trust in Detroit in the early 1930s. While holidays provided Mrs. Wilson the opportunity to have a party, she also found great pleasure in planning parties for a variety of occasions, including a special one for a housewarming at Meadow Brook Hall, to which she invited 850 guests; she wore a magnificent lemon-yellow gown sprinkled with cut-velvet flowers that flowed onto a small train. At this time, she was

**ABOVE:** *Eggs the colors of Jordan almonds, held in an Edwardian silver egg cruet, could herald Easter morning, whether being served by a waiter at The Greenbrier, or to one's delighted children at home.*

*A lovingly set table for an Easter or Mother's Day luncheon at The Whitney uses delicate mauves and amethysts and a centerpiece of forced freesias. Cupids add to the romantic blending of George Jones 1910 gilded plates with an entire service of Steuben glassware. Reed & Barton's 1899 Love Adorned flatware adds to the femininity of the mood, as do the antique linen cut-work tablecloth and pleated silk napkins.*

forty-six years old and had been married to Alfred Wilson for four years. For a surprise party for her daughter's twenty-fifth birthday, Mrs. Wilson had the dining-room table set with a solid-gold dinner service on a Venetian lace tablecloth, and she hired Tommy Dorsey and his twenty-two-piece band to play in the ballroom. Whereas her sister-in-law, Anna Thompson Dodge (whose husband, Horace, had died, as had Matilda's first husband, John, during the influenza epidemic in 1920), relished her place as a society figure, Matilda Dodge Wilson sought refuge from the glare of public life.

The many silver pieces made for the express purpose of serving wine and champagne make it easy for even the novice to present such beverages with an air of sophistication that belies a lack of experience. The Art Nouveau period, in particular, yields to us a great wealth of serving pieces, decorated with its characteristic swirls and exaggerated botanical motifs. Champagne flutes are perhaps the most delicate of all glasses, with their bowls pirouetting on slender stems like graceful ballerinas performing in *Swan Lake*. A footed silver bowl might hold some dainty champagne grapes dusted with sugar, while Sheffield silver trays and champagne coolers provide just the right touch of elegance. Many people like to use large pieces, such as punch bowls, to serve as bases for holiday centerpieces—their depth is perfect for securing greens or flowers in frogs, as well as giving ample room for plenty of water to keep everything fresh. Epergnes also make splendid centerpieces, particularly at Thanksgiving; like a graceful hand holding a bunch of fresh eucalyptus and bittersweet, epergnes were commonly used on Victorian and Edwardian tables, and they can make even contemporary table settings take on a refined air.

Although many holidays are celebrated on the same day by every-

one, they are rarely observed in the same way, for families create their own unique holiday traditions that are lovingly played out over and over again every year, establishing a comfortable familiarity. Some families always decorate their Christmas tree on the same day, in the same room, with treasured ornaments that have lasted generations, and such traditions, which are many years in the making, hold fast, and are often handed down from one generation to the next. The funny little party games that loving aunts and uncles devised for us when we were small (to keep us occupied and out of trouble while the turkey was carved or the cakes and cookies were cooling) somehow end up being played at our own holiday parties by our children—such continuity helps keep the thread of family strong and unbroken.

While Christmas and New Year's Eve certainly are the most eagerly awaited holidays of the year, anticipated and planned for well in advance, their dazzle should not be allowed to blind us to the possibilities of doing the other holidays in great style. Easter and Mother's Day, although quieter celebrations, are opportunities to use colors like mauve and lilac to create tables of great beauty. Steuben's pale amethyst etched glasses filled with spring wine, together with a service of George Jones mauve china and Bavarian plates embossed in gold and silver, could be used to create a memorable table for an Easter luncheon. Guests might enjoy raspberry sorbet with 1899 Reed and Barton silver dessert spoons in the Love Adorned pattern while watching the Easter Parade on television or the wonderful movie *Easter Parade* with Fred Astaire and Judy Garland.

*OPPOSITE AND BELOW: A small but grand Thanksgiving dinner features Copeland Spode china gaily decorated with hand-painted fowl and a table filled with a variety of sparkling Tiffin colored glass and initialed ivory napkin rings for each guest. A Tiffany chandelier highlights the intricate carving on a built-in sideboard in The Whitney's original 1894 formal dining room.*

At Meadow Brook Hall, which was a working farm with one thousand laying hens and a huge flock of turkeys, one can be fairly certain that, given such a wealth of eggs, Easter must have been a favorite holiday. Easter eggs are often displayed on bright green plastic grass tucked into plastic baskets, and that is truly a shame—with just a minimum of extra trouble the eggs, which take so long to dye and decorate, could be shown off on some real grass, grown from fast-growing seed and displayed in either cut-glass or silver bowls.

Easter was very much the time to be seen at The Greenbrier. As the society writer Cholly Knickerbocker noted in 1926, "The Easter parade on Fifth Avenue is becoming obsolete to society, as fashion dictates leaving town. It is 'the thing' to pass Easter-tide at The Greenbrier." At the resort today, guests there on their Easter vacation might find themselves treated to colorful eggs served in a silver egg cruet on a tray decorated with graceful swans. As with all things, it is the fine details that make the difference between the mundane and the marvelous.

For Mother's Day, a centerpiece of sweetly scented freesia or tuberose and a bottle of Moët et Chandon for toasting to a mother's good health and happiness would make any woman proud that she raised a child thoughtful enough to create such a lovely table for her special day.

**BELOW:** *A handsome silver and inlaid mahogany gallery tray holds an Art Nouveau silver bowl, pitcher, and chased lily-pad Martelé jug, all made by Gorham between 1900 and 1905, which would add to the abundance of Thanksgiving.*

**LEFT:** *At Cranbrook a German Jugendstil repoussé silver punch bowl holds a stunning array of fall foliage gathered from the garden to create a splendid centerpiece.*

**BELOW:** *For the Thanksgiving sideboard a treasure of silver figural serving pieces captures the essence of different decorative-arts movements. Reindeer enhance an 1890s Gorham soup tureen and a 1920s punch bowl with a glass liner by Baccarat. The silver covered-chalice drinking cup with the fish finial was made in 1914 in London by Omar Ramsden.*

While some affluent families during the 1910s, 1920s, and 1930s played a seasonal version of society hopscotch—skipping from Newport and Saratoga in the summer to the Berkshires in October, to either The Greenbrier in West Virginia or the Grand Hotel on Lake Michigan for Thanksgiving, to Palm Beach, Florida, or Del Coronado, California, for the winter, with a New Year's cruise to parts sunny and southerly— then, as now, for many of us there is no place like home for the holidays. Airports are jammed, highways are clogged, and telephone lines are tied up during the holidays with people seeking white Christmases just like the ones they used to know. No matter how advanced our communications systems get, there is nothing that can actually compare to being there in the flesh to watch loved ones tear open meticulously wrapped packages or hold up a glass in a warm toast to the New Year, a new baby, or a newlywed couple.

In early December, Matilda Dodge Wilson would leave Meadow Brook Hall in Detroit and head for the wilds of Fifth Avenue in New York to do her Christmas shopping, but would return home in plenty of time to spend evenings writing out holiday cards and wrapping presents with her family. Matilda and her husband, Alfred Wilson, often had sleigh-riding parties, to which they invited friends and neighbors; after an afternoon of sliding down the icy slopes of the estate, it must have been a great joy to return to the warmth of Meadow Brook Hall, with its many fireplaces blazing and the exhilarating sound of carols being played on their Aeolian organ. A ceiling-high Christmas tree graced the living room, while two more trees, one in the entrance and one in the servants' hall, displayed traditional ornaments that Matilda Wilson generously gave away to visiting children. Poinsettias and holiday greens gathered from the estate's many evergreen trees decorated the hall's huge staircase and knitted and needlepoint stockings were carefully hung from the mantels.

**OPPOSITE:** *After the tree has been trimmed at Meadow Brook Hall, a Christmas Eve dinner that breaks tradition by not using the traditional red and green blends Royal Doulton's gilded lavender dinner service with elegant lavender Steuben wine and Cambridge gold-overlay pink glasses, and gold vermeil serving pieces embellished with celluloid handles. A gold Pickard fluted bowl and Baccarat bronze d'oré lusters add a further glow to the holiday table.*

A hearty breakfast was always planned for Christmas morning, when a family employee dressed as Santa Claus would make an appearance to the delight of children and adults alike. Later in the day, after a frosty horse-drawn sleigh ride, the family would sit down for a turkey dinner with all the trimmings. The dining-room table's centerpiece was a small sleigh modeled after the family's real one, filled to overflowing with small, elaborately wrapped gifts from which strings were extended—each child was allowed, in turn, to pull three strings, retrieving three boxes filled with small gifts such as pens, charms, jewelry, or watches.

New Year's Eve was a favorite party time at Meadow Brook Hall as well. Friends were invited over for cocktails and a lobster-and-champagne supper; the last, treasured hours of the fading year were spent singing and dancing until a rousing toast of Tom and Jerrys ushered in the New Year—all of this merriment was followed by game after game of bridge, usually lasting until four or five in the morning.

In keeping with the traditional mood embraced by many families during the holidays, certain favorite wineglasses, serving platters, or splendid pieces of silver seem to show up on the dinner, lunch, or brunch table whenever jingle bells ring and Easter eggs roll. Today, in our frenetic world where nothing seems to stay the same for more than two days in a row, there is something to be said for knowing that our grandmother's punch bowl bearing her monogram will be set, front and center, on the Christmas table, and will be filled with eggnog, and that her mother's cut-glass vase and special china will grace the sideboard for cookies and coffee on New Year's Day.

**OPPOSITE AND FOLLOW-
ING PAGES:** *A time and place with which to celebrate the very first minute of a brand-new year is in the grand entrance hall at Meadow Brook, toasting the moment with a set of monogrammed harlequin Czechoslovakian champagnes, or French crystal flutes, which are served from a massive refectory table that displays some of the house's collection of English silver, including a glorious five-arm candelabra, punch bowl, and tray. A grapevine-patterned cooler holds greens that not only contribute color but also give a festive scent to the hall.*

# ACKNOWLEDGMENTS

Perhaps because half of this book was photographed in Los Angeles, I feel like one of those often unknown Oscar recipients who pull out a long list of people to thank, while I, the audience, groan impatiently, waiting to move on to the next award. Now I can commiserate with their plight, hoping that I've remembered everyone who made this book a reality. So, in the interest of page time, let's begin the roll call.

Starting with the lean, mean "team of three" who brought the photos to life, in three city locations. Thanks to Joshua Greene, co-author, photographer, and friend, whose eager willingness to "go beyond" motivated us at each day's location. He never failed to surprise us with new lighting techniques that added warmth and depth, and illuminated new perspectives in our tabletop visual histories. His images bring us and the reader into the frame, and always make us feel that we have been seated at the best table in the house.

To Sara Scott Cullen, our Detroit interior designer–turned–photo stylist, whose unerring eye for color and innovative details kept the settings as fresh as the spectacular flowers she selected and arranged at each location. With great good humor she kept us moving along to accomplish more than we hoped for each day. Leaving her clients and "day job" in Detroit, she graciously joined us in California, providing this book with its continuous visual flow.

To Marilyn Avratin, who literally "moved mountains" of antiques and merchandise, unpacking and repacking as many as thirty huge boxes a day, as things were routed in and out of locations. Keeping track and in control of special pieces, and miraculously returning all in perfect condition were daunting tasks accomplished with unfailing energy, expertise, and good nature. She is my right hand whether on special photo assignments, working year-round back at my shop, The Country Dining Room Antiques in Great Barrington, Massachusetts, or helping me with all the details and editing this book.

The backup team in the shop became off-site facilitators who enabled us to get the job done. My husband, Mike Chefetz, responded to every need and call, offering tireless help, support, and encouragement. Tom Hayes made welcome styling and copy suggestions, and kept our business going in the shop. Korina Gambino was the mighty little one who did the packing, unpacking, and listing of fifty-plus boxes at home base, and mailed things to us overnight when emergencies arose.

On the receiving end, Mary Jane Shannon, owner of the Blanche House Bed and Breakfast in Detroit, and my daughter and son-in-law, Tarin and Joshua Wilson, in whose house I stayed in Los Angeles, were graciously forbearing as mountains of packing boxes cluttered up their vestibules each day.

From Joshua's end, thanks go to his backup team at the Milton H. Greene archives in Florence, Oregon. They were led by Sophie Kage, who also doubled as our creative stylist at The Greenbrier Hotel, and include Carol and her staff at Carol Color Lab in New York, who provided care and expertise in processing all of our film.

Finally, making sure we were fully insured and therefore able to borrow priceless objects and to photograph in historical locations, Mark Selkowitz and Kim Knights of Colt Insurance in Pittsfield once again came to the rescue.

So far, my thanks have centered on the photographic aspects of this book, and while the photographs certainly provide the initial attraction and visual feast, in the end, the written word serves up the mental nourishment, the main course of information that gives insight to the splendid visuals. My wholehearted thanks to Risa Palazzo, whose gracefully descriptive words in every way met the challenge of Joshua's dramatic images. With a zest for uncovering new insights and information, Risa was a joy to work with, with her on-time professionalism and willingness to listen to suggestions.

I have our agents, Gayle Benderoff and Deborah Geltman, to thank for suggesting Risa to me, and Gayle in particular to thank for sticking with me and this book through many changes and false starts. Above all, I was thankful, grateful, and blessed by Sarah Scheffel's arrival at Penguin Studio as the editor who got this project under way. Her initial enthusiasm and support, followed by Cyril Nelson's final editing and knowledge of the decorative arts, guided us in our efforts to produce a "first-class" book. For visualizing just that, we thank our designer Renato Stanisic and Jaye Zimet, our art director at Penguin. Thanks to Christopher Sweet for solving the title mystery. We're also grateful to Michael Fragnito, our publisher, for believing in our first book, *Antiques for the Table,* and for keeping it in print (it's now in its fourth printing), thus allowing it to find a wide and appreciative audience. Thanks to Susan Williams, whose invaluable historic insight added to this book as well as to our first.

The next group to acknowledge is my "scouts," those diligent ladies and gentlemen who made location suggestions, set up appointments, and opened some marvelous doors. Our test shoot at The Greenbrier was facilitated by Sharon Rowe, Director of Public Relations, and by Betsy Conte, Social Director, who enlisted the aid of chefs, waiters, and bellmen to fill our plates and move our merchandise on time.

In Detroit, there were many scouts, but the two who started it all in motion were Wendy Jennings and Susie MacMillan, business partners who produce a series of antiques shows in Michigan and Ohio, and arranged for my Columbus, Ohio, Birmingham, Alabama, and Grosse Pointe, Michigan, lectures. At dinner with Wendy I met Ron Fox of the Whitney and Van Dyke Place restaurants, and it was his vast collec-

tions of tableware antiques, and his beautifully restored restaurants, with their authentic period interiors, that made me decide, that night, that the book had to begin right there in Detroit. Additional thanks to Ron's partners, Richard Kughn and John McCarthy. Through Janette Engelhardt and Jan Mann, co-chairs of the Birmingham Community House Antiques Show, I met Kathy O'Connell, who had engineered the meeting with Ron, and kindly "chauffeured" me to view many wonderful private homes, as well as the stunning Cranbrook Academy. It was Janette's inspired suggestion that we stop to visit Sara Cullen's charming house, which led to Sara's position as our stylist par excellence, and she in turn opened the door to Tom Verwest's special environment.

Our thanks to Meadow Brook Hall's Lisa Baylis Ashby, Director, and Corenna Aldrich, Public Relations Director, for quickly deciding to allow us to photograph there. Thanks to Director John Miller, Curator Maureen Devine, and her assistant Josephine Shea, who made our work easier at the Edsel and Eleanor Ford house. Special thanks to Karen Serota, who gave up a Saturday so this book could include photographs of Cranbrook House as well as Saarinen House, both part of Cranbrook Academy, where Director Gregory Wittkopp graciously allowed our efforts.

The scouting team in Los Angeles included Joyce MacRae (whom I called at Gep Durenberger's welcome suggestion), whose knowledge of Los Angeles—area houses and neighborhoods is astounding; the enormously helpful Dawn Moore, the Manager of Christofle; Suzanne Rheinstein of Hollyhock; and Kelly McLeod, Phoebe Vaccaro, Lucy Webb, and Marcia Ziffren. Thanks to them, and to the following for allowing us to photograph their private houses and collections: Tony Duquette, Jane and Joe Fehrenbacher, Harriet and Richard Gold, Curtis Harrington, Jeffrey Herr and Christopher Molinar, Linda and

Stewart Resnick and their staff members Bernard Jazzar and Jerry Castillo, Joel Silver, Ruth and Hutton Wilkinson, and Marcia and Kenneth Ziffren. A special acknowledgment must also be made to Ivo Hadjiev, the Virginia Robinson House's living historian and majordomo, who charmed us with his recollections of Mrs. Robinson, her parties, and visitors to the house and incredible gardens. For their unfailing patience, adaptability, and "let's do it" attitude, we all thank the directors, curators, and accommodating staff at the public historic houses that add authenticity to our tabletop view of life between 1890 and 1940; they include the Friends of The Virginia Robinson House and Garden, Melissa Patten at The Lanterman House, Mary Ceballos at The Oviatt Penthouse, Virginia Kazor and Jan Kolb at Hollyhock House, Tom Bosley and Bobbi Mapstone at The Gamble House, and Elizabeth Borsting, Ron Smith, and their assistants, Anthony Vargas and Brian Howell, on board the *Queen Mary*. I believe the best way to thank them is with the locations of historic places (see page 235), which lists phone numbers with which to verify seasonal visiting days and hours, and a brief description of each property and its significant features. Another great asset was Susan Brown Draudt, who, as she also did for our first book, provided food-styling services at our Pasadena-area locations when we were on a very tight schedule. In addition, the chefs and staff at The Whitney, Van Dyke Place, and *Queen Mary* restaurants added their artistry to many of our photographs.

Finally, the antiques and other objects that we had the pleasure of photographing in twenty-three locations were more often than not lent to us by a variety of sources. In addition to the tableware, antiques, and vast array of linens that came from my shop, much came from renowned New York City sources, many of whom were also lenders listed in *Antiques for the Table*. (There's a star next to their names in the retail source list beginning on page 237.) In the Detroit and Los Angeles areas many other dealers and shops filled the gaps, and they, along with Pat Thompson at Replacements in Greensboro, North Carolina, who sourced our needs at The Greenbrier, are in the greatly expanded source list. We thank them all for trusting us with often rare and costly pieces.

There were private individuals who headed our plans and graciously lent us their special treasures and mementos to use in other locations. Included in that group are Karen Catto Armstrong, Claudia Aronow-Roush, Marilyn Avratin, Barbara and Alan Boroff, Lorna Sale Bullis, Constance and David Clapp, Sara Scott Cullen, Ron Fox, Marjorie and Richard Gidman, Arlene Gilman, Harriet Gold, Beverly Grossman, Joan Kaminow, Joe Keenan, Brian Killian, Flann Lippincott, Giles Marsden, Tom Myers, Richard Osterberg, Susan and Bruce Pernick, Lee Sanders, Doris and Michael Simon, D'Janet Strumrieter, Robert Saarinen Swanson, Thelma Turkel, Phoebe Vaccaro, Terri Wilde, Tarin and Joshua Wilson, and Bob Winston. We thank each and every one, including you, the reader, who had the forbearance to stick with me to read these oft-spoken Oscar-times words, "We couldn't have done it without them!"

# BIBLIOGRAPHY

Affron, Matthew, Stephanie Barron, and Sabine Eck-
mann. *Exiles and Emigrés: The Flight of European
Artists from Hitler*. New York: Los Angeles
County Museum of Art and Harry N. Abrams,
1997.

Anscombe, Isabelle. *Arts and Crafts Style*. London:
Phaidon Press, 1991.

Archboldt, Rick, and Dana McCauley. *Last Dinner on
the Titanic*. Toronto: Madison Press Books, 1997.

Aslet, Clive. *The American Country House*. New Haven
and London: Yale University Press, 1990.

Barmeier, Jim. *Manners and Customs*. New York:
Chelsea House, 1997.

Battie, David. *Sotheby's Concise Encyclopedia of Porcelain*. London: Conran Octopus, 1989.

Battie, David, and Michael Turner. *The Price Guide to
19th and 20th Century British Pottery*. Suffolk, England: The Antique Collector's Club, 1979.

Bosley, Edward R. *Gamble House: Greene and Greene*.
London: Phaidon Press, 1992.

Bridenstine, James A. *Edsel and Eleanor Ford House*.
Woodland, Md.: Wolk Press, 1988.

Carpenter, Charles H. *Gorham Silver, 1831–1981*.
New York: Dodd, Mead & Company, 1982.

Conte, Robert S. *The History of The Greenbrier: America's Resort*. Charleston, S.C.: Pictorial Histories
Publishing, 1989.

Curtis, Tony. *Glass and Metalware: Collecting for Pleasure*. London: Bracken Books, 1992.

Dale, Nancy H. *Tiffany Table Settings*. New York:
Thomas Y. Crowell Company, 1960.

Davidson, Marshall B., and Elizabeth Stillinger. *The
American Wing: The Metropolitan Museum of Art*.
New York: Knopf, 1985.

Doby, Georges, and Michelle Perrot. *A History of
Women*. Boston: Harvard University Press, 1996.

Douglas, George H. *All Aboard! The Railroad in American Life*. New York: Marlowe & Company, 1992.

Eberle, Linda, and Susan Scott. *The Charlton Standard
Catalogue of Chintz*. Toronto: W. K. Cross, 1996.

Evans, Sarah M. *Born for Liberty*. New York: Simon &
Schuster, 1997.

Fahr-Becker, Gabrielle. *Wiener Werkstätte,
1903–1932*. Koln: Benedict Taschen Verlag,
1995.

Florence, Gene. *Stemware Identification, 1920–1960*.
Paducah, Ky.: Collector Books, 1997.

———. *Very Rare Glassware of the Depression Years*. Paducah, Ky.: Collector Books, 1997.

Frost, Elizabeth, and Kathryn Cullen-DuPont.
*Women's Suffrage in America*. Oxford: Roundhouse
Publishing, 1992.

Gleeson, Janet. *Collecting Pottery and Porcelain*. London: Reed International Books, 1997.

Gombrich, E. H. *The Story of Art*. London: Phaidon
Press, 1995.

Griffin, Leonard, Louis K. Meisel, and Susan Pear
Meisel. *Clarice Cliff: The Bizarre Affair*. London:
Thames and Hudson, 1988.

Hannah, Frances. *Ceramics: Twentieth-Century Design*.
New York: E. P. Dutton, 1986.

Hill, Susan. *The Shelley Style*. Warwickshire, England:
Jazz Publications, 1990.

Hoffmann, Donald. *Frank Lloyd Wright's Hollyhock
House*. New York: Dover Publications, 1992.

Hogg, Min, and Wendy Harrop. *Interiors*. New York:
Clarkson N. Potter, 1988.

Jasper, Joanne. *Turn of the Century American Dinnerware, 1880s to 1920s*. Augora Hills, Calif.:
Schroeder Publishing Co., 1996.

Jenkins, Emyl. *Emyl Jenkins' Reproduction Furniture*.
New York: Crown Publishers, 1995.

Knight, Arthur, and Eliot Elisofon. *The Hollywood
Style*. London: Macmillan, 1969.

Knowles, Eric. *Victoriana to Art Deco*. London: Reed
International Books, 1993.

Lind, Carla. *Frank Lloyd Wright's California Houses*. San Francisco: Pomegranate Artbooks, 1995.

———. *Frank Lloyd Wright's Dining Rooms*. San Francisco: Pomegranate Artbooks, 1995.

Maillard, Jacqueline, and Pascal Hinous. *Histoires de Tables*. Paris: Flammarion, 1989.

Mayer, Barbara. *In the Arts and Crafts Style*. San Francisco: Chronicle Books, 1993.

Mennell, Stephen. *All Manners of Food*. Oxford, England: Basil Blackwell, 1985.

Miller, Martin, and Judith Miller. *Understanding Antiques*. London: Reed International Books, 1989.

Miller, Muriel. *Collecting Royal Winton Chintz*. London: Francis Joseph Publications, 1996.

Myerson, Jeremy, and Sylvia Katz. *Conran Design Guides: Tableware*. New York: Van Nostrand Reinhold, 1990.

Osterberg, Richard. *Silver Hollowware for Dining Elegance*. Atglen, Pa.: Schiffer Publishing, 1994.

———. *Sterling Silver Flatware for Dining Elegance*. Atglen, Pa.: Schiffer Publishing, 1994.

Pina, Leslie. *Pottery: Modern Wares, 1920–1960*. Atglen, Pa.: Schiffer Publishing, 1994.

Page, Bob, and Dale Frederiksen. *A Collection of American Crystal*. Greensboro, N.C.: Page-Frederiksen Publishing Company, 1995.

———. *Seneca Glass Company, 1891–1983*. Greensboro, N.C.: Page-Frederiksen Publishing Company, 1995.

———. *Tiffin Is Forever*. Greensboro, N.C.: Page-Frederiksen Publishing Company, 1994.

Paston-Williams, Sara. *The Art of Dining: A History of Cooking and Eating*. New York: Harry N. Abrams, 1993.

Payne, Christopher. *Sotheby's Concise Encyclopedia of Furniture*. London: Conran Octopus, 1989.

Plante, Ellen M. *The Victorian House*. New York: Michael Friedman Publishing Group, 1995.

Russell, John. *The Meanings of Modern Art*. New York: Harper & Row, 1981.

Spours, Judy. *Art Deco Tableware*. London: Ward Lock Publications, 1988.

Street-Porter, Tim. *The Los Angeles House*. New York: Clarkson N. Potter, 1995.

Thomas, Jeanette A. *Images of the Gamble House: Masterwork of Greene and Greene*. Los Angeles: Balcony Press, 1989.

Venable, Charles L. *Silver in America, 1840–1940*. New York: Harry N. Abrams, 1994.

Visser, Margaret. *The Rituals of Dinner*. New York: Penguin Books, 1992.

Wels, Susan. *Titanic: Legacy of the World's Greatest Ocean Liner*. New York: Time Life Books, 1997.

Welsh, Joe, and Mike Schafer. *Classic American Streamliners*. Osceola, Wis.: Motorbooks International, 1997.

Wittkopp, Gregory. *Saarinen House and Garden: A Total Work of Art*. New York: Harry N. Abrams, 1995.

Wolfman, Peri, and Charles Gold. *Forks, Knives, and Spoons*. New York: Clarkson N. Potter, 1994.

Wirth, Barbara, and Pascal Hinous. *The Elegant Table*. New York: Harry N. Abrams, 1987.

# LOCATIONS

**HISTORICAL SITES OPEN
TO THE PUBLIC
THE BANNING RESIDENCE
MUSEUM**
401 East M Street
Wilmington, CA 90748
310-548-7777
A Greek Revival house built for General
Phineas Banning in 1864, this house, with
its original furnishings, is one of the oldest
standing wooden residences in Southern
California.

**CRANBROOK HOUSE AND
GARDENS**
1221 North Woodward Avenue
P.O. Box 801
Bloomfield Hills, MI 48303-0801
248-645-3311
Situated on 40 acres within the 325-acre
Cranbrook Educational Community,
Cranbrook House was designed by
noted architect Albert Kahn for George
Booth, publisher of the *Detroit Evening
News,* and his wife, Ellen, who began
residence at Cranbrook House, an
English-style manor, in 1908.
Cranbrook achieved distinction among
American estates by commissioning the
finest artisans, craftsmen, and studios of
the period to embellish the house and its
grounds with outstanding Arts and
Crafts design. George Booth created the
original landscaping, which continues to
evolve today.

**THE EDSEL AND ELEANOR
FORD HOUSE**
110 Lake Shore Drive
Grosse Pointe Shores, MI 48236
313-884-4222
The stately fifty-two-room Cotswold-
style mansion designed by architect
Albert Kahn reflects the Fords' love of
art in many forms, and it preserves for
posterity fine examples of English
paneling of the sixteenth, seventeenth,
and eighteenth centuries. The
magnificent grounds, designed by Jens
Jensen, will lead you to the breathtaking

gardens, the enchanting Play House, the
Pool, the Pool House, and the Gate
Lodge Garage, where Mrs. Ford's 1952
Lincoln Town Car is on display.

**THE GAMBLE HOUSE**
4 Westmorland Place
Pasadena, CA 91103-3593
626-793-3334
Built for Procter and Gamble heir David
B. Gamble in 1908 by two brothers from
Ohio, architects Charles and Henry
Greene, whose Craftsman-style houses
and interior furnishings, an outgrowth of
Arts and Crafts philosophy, were
masterpieces of Japanese-inspired
detailing, crafted like a fine piece of
furniture. The Gamble House represents
the finest example of the Greenes'
distinctive architectural style, with the
original furnishings and stained glass
windows still intact.

**THE GREENBRIER**
300 West Main Street
White Sulphur Springs, WV 24986
304-536-1110
Throughout the nineteenth century, The
Greenbrier was *the* southern summer
resort. Guests came to use the mineral
water, to enjoy the mountain climate, and
to mingle with the famous of the day.
Today many of the original cottages are
preserved as guest accommodations,
although enlarged and modernized. In
1913, the central Georgian section of The
Greenbrier opened on a year-round basis,
with golf and tennis as featured
attractions. Subsequent additions to this
National Historic Landmark have refined
the hotel's architecture to reflect the
colonial Virginia style.

**HOLLYHOCK HOUSE
THE BARNSDALL
FOUNDATION**
4800 Hollywood Boulevard
Los Angeles, CA 90027
213-662-7272
Hollyhock House was the first Los Angeles

project of America's most famous
architect, Frank Lloyd Wright. Built
between 1919 and 1921, it represents his
earliest efforts to develop a regionally
appropriate style of architecture for
Southern California. The house takes its
name from the favorite flower of Wright's
client, oil heiress Aline Barnsdall. At her
request, hollyhocks were incorporated into
the decorative features of the house, with
stylized representations of the flower found
on the roofline, walls, columns, planters,
and furniture.

**THE LANTERMAN HOUSE**
4420 Encinas Drive
La Canada, CA 91011
818-790-1421
In 1914, Dr. Ray Lanterman and his wife,
Emily, built this Craftsman-style home,
which they called El Retiro. The house is a
veritable time capsule of early-twentieth-
century California life.

**THE LOS ANGELES
CONSERVANCY**
523 West Sixth Street
Los Angeles, CA 90014
213-623-2489
An organization dedicated to the
recognition and preservation of the
historical architectural resources of
Greater Los Angeles, offering conducted
walking tours.

**MEADOW BROOK HALL**
Oakland University
Rochester, MI 48309
248-370-3140
After visiting castles and manor houses in
England with American architect William
E. Kapp, Matilda Dodge Wilson and her
husband, Alfred, commissioned him to
design and build their 100-room Tudor-
style home, Meadow Brook Hall. In
1926, ground was broken on the Dodge
property in the rolling hills of Rochester
farmland, and despite the English style of
the house Mrs. Wilson took great pride
in it as an American product built almost

entirely of native materials, using American artists and craftsmen. Although it was architecturally imposing, and contained priceless furnishings, the house, which was completed in 1929, was never a museum. It was built as a family home, filled with items Mrs. Wilson liked for the warmth and interest they added to the Hall.

**THE OVIATT PENTHOUSE**
617 South Olive, Suite 1210
Los Angeles, CA 90014
213-622-6096
This 1927 penthouse, built atop the downtown Los Angeles building bearing his name, was the fashionable Art Deco home and business address of James Oviatt, a noted menswear retailer, who commissioned the largest installation of Lalique glassware outside France. Mirrors, windows, panels, lighting, and fixtures are still intact in this stylish space, which can be rented for private parties, movie sets, and photo shoots.

**QUEEN MARY HOTEL**
1126 Queen's Highway
Long Beach, CA 90802
562-435-3511
The *Queen Mary* had its maiden voyage in 1936 and was the sleek modern star of the Cunard Line. During World War II, it served as a troopship, and was later restored to its former splendor to sail in the 1950s. Today, owned by the City of Long Beach, the *Queen Mary* serves as a hotel where guests relive the travel experience of less hurried times, and can

take guided tours of the vessel from the captain's bridge to the boiler room. With many fine restaurants and ballrooms this is a favorite venue for private parties, special events, and conferences.

**THE VIRGINIA ROBINSON HOUSE AND GARDENS**
1008 Elden Way
Beverly Hills, CA 90210
310-276-3302
In 1911, department-store heir Harry Robinson and his bride, Virginia, built their home on six acres at the highest point of then-undeveloped Beverly Hills. Their new residence was a wedding gift from the house's architect, Mrs. Robinson's father, Nathaniel Dryden. Landscape designer Charles Gibbs Adams later transformed the open hillside into a private paradise of exotic terraced gardens surrounding the classic Mediterranean-style villa, filled with mementos of the Robinsons' extensive travels and famous guests. This house is listed in The National Register of Historic Places.

**SAARINEN HOUSE**
1221 North Woodward Avenue
P.O. Box 801
Bloomfield Hills, MI 48303-0801
248-645-3311

Designed by Finland's most renowned architect, Eliel Saarinen, in 1930, this visionary modern American residence and its furnishings are a testament to the endurance and influence of his teaching at Cranbrook Academy, where the architect

lived in a community of artists and designers who worked and taught under the patronage of George Booth.

**VAN DYKE PLACE RESTAURANT**
649 Van Dyke Avenue
Detroit, MI 48214
313-821-2620
Singled out in 1912 by *Town and Country* magazine as "House of the Year," this French-inspired eighteen-room building is a fine example of Beaux-Arts Revivalism in its architecture and detailing. Once the home of William Muir Finck, a wealthy clothing manufacturer, it is now a fine landmark restaurant.

**THE WHITNEY RESTAURANT**
4421 Woodward Avenue
Detroit, MI 48201
313-832-5700
The fifty-two-room Whitney mansion, completed in 1894, was designed for lumber baron David Whitney, Jr., and called by one newspaper article in 1894 "the most elaborate and substantial residence in this part of the country." Created in the Romanesque Revival style by Detroit architect Gordon W. Lloyd, the mansion is built of pink granite, which gives the outside of the house a striking rose hue. In the great hall, a grand staircase with a bronze balustrade is illuminated by richly colored Tiffany stained-glass panels on the second and third floors. This landmark house is now a renowned restaurant.

# SOURCES

**AMPHORA ARTS
AND ANTIQUES**
308 North Rodeo Drive
Beverly Hills, CA 90210
310-273-4222
China, glass, silver
*pages 4, 5, 115, 159*

**BERGDORF
GOODMAN**
754 Fifth Avenue
New York, NY 10019
212-753-7300
Seventh-floor home furnishings
and antiques department
Kentshire Galleries, L'Hotel,
English China Boutique, Gold
& White Shop
*pages 81, 82, 168, 169*

**BAKER, KNAPP &
TUBBS**
Michigan Design Center,
Suite 60
1700 Stutz Drive
Troy, MI 48048
810-649-6730
Furniture, fabrics, decorative
objects
*pages 65, 214*

**NANCY BROUS**
1008 Lexington Avenue
New York, NY 10021
212-772-7515
martini shakers and decorative
accessories
*page 178*

**THE CHINTZ
COLLECTOR**
600 Columbia Street
Pasadena, CA 91105
626-441-4708
Antique Chintz wares
*pages 118–121*

**CHRISTOFLE**
9515 Brighton Way
Beverly Hills, CA 90210
310-858-8058
Silver, glass
*pages 55–57, 78, 79, 85, 146,
147, 216, 217*

**\*THE COUNTRY
DINING ROOM
ANTIQUES**
178 Main Street
Great Barrington, MA 01230
413-528-5050
China, glass, silver, linens,
accessories
*pages 4, 8, 12, 18, 29, 35, 37, 54,
66, 69, 71, 73, 75, 85, 106, 110,
115, 117, 128, 132, 139, 151,
161, 171, 176, 192, 208, 217,
221*

**"DAINTY BLUE"
ANTIQUES AND
COLLECTIBLES**
General Delivery
North Truro, MA 02652
508-487-0902
Shelley and Calyx ware
*pages 100, 101*

**DECO DELUXE**
993 Lexington Avenue
New York, NY 10021
212-472-7222
Antique glass, silver, china
*pages 178, 179, 182*

**DEL GIUDICE
ANTIQUES**
515 S. Lafayette
Royal Oak, MI 48067
248-399-2608
*pages 9, 38, 65*

**TONY DUQUETTE**
P.O. Box 69858
Beverly Hills, CA 90069
310-271-3574

Artist/Designer
*pages 150-52, 154*

**KRISTEN CATTO
ARMSTRONG**
Michigan Design Center,
Suite 108
1700 Stutz Drive
Troy, MI 48084
248-649-6866
English antiques
*page 74*

**\*FORTUNOFF**
681 Fifth Avenue
New York, NY 10022
212-758-6660
Antique silver and silverplate
*pages 15, 59, 220*

**JUDY FRANKEL &
ASSOC.**
2900 West Maple Road,
Suite 111
Troy, MI 48084
248-649-4399
Antiques, decorative objects
*page 105*

**GARDNER & BARR,
INC.**
213 East 60th Street
New York, NY 10022
212-752-0555
Antique Venetian glass
*pages 18, 19, 75, 108, 109*

**\*GORHAM, INC.**
P.O. Box 6150
Providence, RI 02917
401-333-4360
Silver
*pages 161, 210*

**HISTORICAL
DESIGN**
306 East 61st Street
New York, NY 10021
212-593-4528

Antique china, glass
*pages 78, 79*

**\*HOFFMAN-
GAMPETRO
ANTIQUES**
1050 Second Avenue
New York, NY 10022
212-758-1252
China, glass, silver
*pages 28, 75, 156, 157, 207, 215*

**HOLLYHOCK**
218 North Larchmont
Boulevard
Los Angeles, CA 90048
213-931-3400
Decorative objects, antiques,
china

**INTERIOR SPACE
ALIGNMENT/TOM
VERWEST**
1387 Club Drive
Bloomfield Hills,
MI 48302-0823
248-332-5853
Interior design
*pages 45, 187, 188, 194*

**IRIS COTTAGE**
P.O. Box 254
Canaan, NY 12029
518-781-4379
Antique pressed glass
*pages 38, 128, 129*

**JAMES II
GALLERIES**
15 East 57th Street
New York, NY 10022
212-355-7040
Antique china, glass, decorative
accessories
*pages 22, 23*

**\*KENTSHIRE
GALLERIES**
37 East 12th Street
New York, NY 10003
212-673-6644
Antique silver, china, glass,
furniture
*pages 11, 161, 178, 185, 220*

**\*ALICE KWARTLER**
123 East 57th Street
New York, NY 10022
212-752-3590
Antique china, glass, silver
*pages 15, 75*

**LALIQUE**
317 North Rodeo Drive
Los Angeles, CA 90210
310-271-7892
Glass, stemware, decorative
objects
*pages 176, 177*

**MICHELE C.
ANTIQUES**
316 South Robertson
Boulevard
Los Angeles, CA 90048
310-246-1759
China, decorative accessories
*pages 208, 209*

**NELSON AND
NELSON ANTIQUES,
INC.**
445 Park Avenue
New York, NY 10022
210-980-5825
Silver, silverplate, glass
*pages 26, 27, 181*

**CHRISTOPHER
OSTAFIN AND
ASSOCIATES**
150 West 25th Street,
Suite 1201
New York, NY 10001
212-352-9210
Antique china, glass
*pages 81, 82*

**RICHARD
OSTERBERG**
1726 West San Medele Avenue
Fresno, CA 93711-2929
209-438-6336
Art Nouveau silver
*pages 6, 7, 20*

**PASADENA
ANTIQUES CENTER
AND ANNEX**
480 and 444 South Oaks
Avenue
Pasadena, CA 91105
818-449-7706
Glass, china, silver
*page 31*

**\*REED & BARTON**
41 Madison Avenue
New York, NY 10010
1-800-822-1824
Silver
*pages 18, 19, 75, 214, 215*

**REPLACEMENTS,
LTD.**
1089 Knox Road
Greensboro, NC 57420-6029
1-800-562-4462
Glass, china, silver
*pages 126, 134, 135, 187*

**RESIDENCE BIS**
4464 West Adams Boulevard
Los Angeles, CA 90016
213-731-9991
Antique china, silver, linens,
furniture

**ROOM WITH A VIEW**
1600 Montana Avenue
Santa Monica, CA 90403
310-998-5858
Linens, glass, flatware
*pages 118, 120, 159, 216, 217*

**SANTA MONICA
ANTIQUE MARKET**
1607 Lincoln Boulevard
Santa Monica, CA 90404
310-314-4899
China, glass, flatware,
decorative accessories
*pages 55–57, 100–102, 113,
216, 217*

**SARA SCOTT
CULLEN DESIGNS**
584 Pleasant Street
Birmingham, MI 48009
810-644-7272
Flowers, containers, glass, props

**\*S.J. SHRUBSOLE
CORP.**
104 East 57th Street
New York, NY 10022
212-753-8920
Antique English silver
*pages 220, 221*

**SUDY'S DESIGNER
LINENS**
110 South Robertson
Boulevard
Los Angeles, CA 90048
310-273-4666
Table and bed linens
*page 125*

**\*TIFFANY & CO.**
Fifth Avenue at 57th Street
New York, NY 10017
212-755-8000
210 North Rodeo Drive
Beverly Hills, CA 90210
310-273-8880
Silver, china, glass
*pages 85, 176, 177, 197*

**TWIN PEAKS**
Village Square, Route 295
East Chatham, NY 12060
518-392-2990
Antique elegant colored
stemware
*pages 19, 26, 66, 141, 156, 157,
171, 183, 186, 200, 201, 207,
218*

**VILLAGE ANTIQUE
CENTER**
P.O. Box 388
Franklin Avenue
Millbrook, NY 12545-0388
914-677-5160
China, glass, silver
*page 73*

**MARTIN WEIL**
Restoration Architect
2175 Cambridge Street
Los Angeles, CA 90006
213-734-9734

**HUTTON
WILKINSON**
P.O. Box 69 A 39
Los Angeles, CA 90069
213-874-7760
Designer
*pages 159, 198, 199*

**WOLFMAN, GOLD
AND GOOD**
117 Mercer Street
New York, NY 10012
212-431-1888
Antique silver

**WOODARD AND
GREENSTEIN**
508 East 74th Street
New York, NY 10021
212-988-2906
Antique china, decorative
accessories

**\*S. WYLER, INC.**
941 Lexington Avenue
New York, NY 10021
212-879-9848
Antique silver and silverplate
*pages 18, 19, 58, 221*